NO RETAKES!

ACTORS & ACTRESSES REMEMBER THE ERA OF LIVE TELEVISION
BY SANDRA GRABMAN AND WRIGHT KING

NO RETAKES! Actors & Actresses Remember the Era of Live Television
©2008 Sandra Grabman & Wright King. All Rights Reserved.
No part of this book may be reproduced in any form or by any means, electronic, mechanical, digital, photocopying or recording, except for the inclusion in a review, without permission in writing from the publisher.

Published in the USA by:
BearManor Media
P O Box 71426
Albany, Georgia 31708
www.bearmanormedia.com

ISBN 1-59393-147-6

Printed in the United States of America.
Book design by Brian Pearce.

TABLE OF CONTENTS

ACKNOWLEDGEMENTS 5

INTRODUCTION BY SANDRA GRABMAN 7

INTRODUCTION BY WRIGHT KING 9

THE DEVELOPMENT OF TELEVISION 17

GETTING THE JOB 35

ON THE JOB 45

AIR TIME! 59

FOR ALL YOU KIDDIES OUT THERE 69

STAY TUNED FOR NEWS 77

IT'S GAME TIME! 81

AND NOW A WORD FROM OUR SPONSOR 87

BLOOPERS 91

THE AUDIENCE 109

MEMORABLE PEOPLE OF THE LIVE TV ERA 115

GOOD-BYE TO THE GOLDEN AGE 123

BIBLIOGRAPHY 129

INDEX 131

ACKNOWLEDGEMENTS

Our profuse thanks go out to the wonderful people listed below for their help. The very familiar names in the "On Stage" category — the performers who have given us such quality entertainment for many years — have been very kind to share their memories with us of working in the exceptional era of live television. The remaining categories list very kind people who have contributed in other ways to bring you this story.

On Stage: Bill Erwin, Kathy Garver, Don Grady, Bill Hayes, Claire Kirby Hooton, Rance Howard, Gloria Jean, Jack Klugman, Steven Marlo, Jan Merlin, Betsy Palmer, Peter Mark Richman, Judy Robinson, Eva Marie Saint, and Chuck Thompson

Cover Models: Jaida Burke, Butch Howard, Steve Howard, Sara Lane, Stacey Lane, Anthony Martorelli, and Robbie Sundberg (with special thanks to Robyn Anthony's of Wallingford, CT, for the setting)

Behind the Spotlights: Madelyn Pugh Davis, Randy and Claudia Ferguson, Phil Grabman, Kathi Law, Loring Mandel, Tim Pennings of WRGB, Rex Strother, and Stone Wallace

Pre-Production: Larry Bloomfield, Joel Blumberg, Rodolfo Carreon, Eric Engberg, Klaus D. Haisch, Richard Holbrook, Peter Anthony Holder, Jeff Howard, Sybil Jason, S. L. Kotar, the Museum of Television & Radio/The Paley Center for Media, Philip Paul, Joe Sarno, and Don Trettel

Post-Production: S. L. Kotar and Ben Ohmart

Cameramen: Jeff Howard (front cover photo) and Keefe Tirral (authors' photo, back cover)

Set Design: Brian Pearce

The Audience: Michael George, Paul Goldsmith, Pamela Greenwood, S. L. Kotar, Jack Lambert, Janet and Roy Marburger, Rev. Marguerite Oetjen, Emily Peters, and Ted Pilonero

INTRODUCTION

BY SANDRA GRABMAN

Remember the good old days when our television fare was broadcast live? Remember when the family comedies and cowboy heroes strove to set a good example for children? Guns in schools were unheard of back then, the drug of choice was aspirin, family units were much stronger, and children respected adults.

They had good reason to all it the "Golden Age of Television." There were only a few networks, so viewers had many shared experiences. A lot of the actors in television dramas had come from vaudeville, radio, and the Broadway stage, and knew how to tell a compelling story. If one of their co-stars missed a line or if a prop failed, they knew how to handle it. Because there were fewer programs aired in any given day, you could be sure the writing and directing would be of the highest caliber, as well.

Books have been written about the history of television and the production challenges, but what about the performers and their audience? What was it like for them?

Actor Wright King was there on our screens during those early days of television when shows were aired live, and he very fondly remembers those wonderful times. His recollections are the foundation of this book. Building on that is my own research that adds such details as specific events, titles, times, places, etc. Interviews with many of Wright's fellow actors and actresses round out the book as they share with us their memories of working on live television.

I hope you will enjoy turning back the calendar to relive with us a magical time in which future superstars were learning their craft while we watched from our living rooms.

INTRODUCTION

BY WRIGHT KING

Television just slipped in there somehow.

In 1940 our high school lecture series included this mathematician who told us someday in the near future, we'd all be sitting in our living rooms watching a new kind of machine, seeing all things that we were listening to now on our radios.

He was right!!!!!!

My Point of View

In May of 1946, World War II was over and I was out of my navy uniform, on the streets of New York City, eager to join the dozens of would-be thespians, fellow vets and others, to prove to all the important producers, directors and agents that I, too, belonged in their world. New York, being the center of theatre and radio, was the place to be. Keeping in touch, I handed a quarter to the news stand guy and picked up my copy of *Actor's Cues*, a weekly, single sheet reporting planned theatre productions as well as information on agents and casting offices, including all addresses. No phoning! You walked. You "made the rounds" - visiting their individual offices, resume in hand. If you were lucky, they eventually called you. I carried out my business on a public phone in the lobby just off my room in a brownstone apartment on West 68th Street.

From time to time, while making my rounds, I became distracted by small gatherings of bystanders in front of shop and bar windows. They seemed quietly transfixed on a small rectangular object in the windows. "What are you doing? What's going on?" I questioned. "Shhhhh," whispered one of the observers, adding while pointing to the object in the window, "They're watching the Dodger game on television." Really? Then I sneaked a look. "Unbelievable," I thought as I returned to my rounds.

Not long afterward, *Actor's Cues* came up with an announcement that plans were underway for televising legitimate theatre. Theatre on a postage stamp? A friend then announced she'd indeed been cast in a drama for *Kraft Television Theatre*. I was able to watch a dress rehearsal of her production. Sheer chaos! It appeared to be a frantically-rehearsed ballet of performers and camera operators wheeling huge boxlike cameras in all directions under the sweltering heat of thousands of watts of illumination. I felt sorry for my friend, happy that I had just signed a contract for a six-month tour in Children's Theatre.

With luck and ambition and a little ushering and serving sodas on the side, I did a stint of being a "super" (supernumerary, supporting actor) in the Yiddish Theatre on Second Avenue, then summer stock, where I earned my Actor's Equity card, leaving New York for a job acting and assistant stage managing in Chicago. Finally, after exactly two years, I was happily back in New York with a great gal, June, my new wife. We were invited to a party, a special event. On our host's new television screen, friends Anthony Quinn and Catherine McCloud were to appear in *Philco Television Playhouse*'s version of a costume classic. The TV screen had grown somewhat, but two fine performers squeezed tightly onto a window too small to accommodate our tiny audience made what I felt was an uncomfortable situation. An interesting concept, but quietly to June I whispered, "I guess I'm just not a pioneer type."

Wright King, live-TV actor

In my absence, along with its publicized growth, came performer union plans and contracts that made appearing "on the air" maybe interesting, at least worth a try. And so when an offer to perform a small role on *What a Life* (aka *The Henry Aldrich Show*, a popular radio presentation recently switched to television), I said okay. The rehearsal for a half-hour episode, though shorter than the theatre rehearsals, took place in the same Malin Studios we were already accustomed to. The rehearsals themselves were not unlike theatre stage, with chalked lines on the floor to designate walls, doors, etc. However, it was the actual broadcast that was decidedly different. Whereas, before, we had an open proscenium and our audiences on the theatre's stage, we now were faced with a large camera, possibly more than one at a time. Wherever you moved you were constantly aware of a camera, and together with quieter voices and subtle gesturing, it seemed at first that you were performing, performing. "Restricted" explained the way

I felt — but, of course, the more rehearsal one had, the easier the whole business of acting was.

I can't remember many actors owning a television set; at this point, it wasn't something that most of us wanted around. So when I did my first *Henry Aldrich* performance, June watched on a neighbor's television set, and June's response was surprisingly positive. She'd personally grown up with *The Henry Aldrich* radio program and was glad to see it come alive on television, liking all the performances. "It's okay in a pinch," I said, happy with my steady theatre job.

Wait a minute…Oh, Sandy just reminded me that it's time to get on with the show, so let's go to our story.

NOTE

To distinguish Wright King's words from those of Sandra Grabman, his memories are set in **bold type** in the following text.

PART ONE

CHAPTER ONE

THE DEVELOPMENT OF TELEVISION

At first, television was not taken seriously.

As it was being developed in the 1920s and 1930s, the public thought it would just be a short-lived novelty. The picture, fuzzy in the earliest years, would sometimes make it quite difficult to figure out what they were seeing. Scientists and engineers all over the world persevered, however, with Philo T. Farnsworth and Vladimir Zworykin in the forefront. Most other technicians were focusing on the spinning-disc theory, but Farnsworth was the one who invented the electronics necessary to make television a commercial success. (Sometimes RCA/NBC* mogul David Sarnoff got the credit, but it was Philo Farnsworth who came up with the idea while in high school and spent the following decades developing television until it was a viable product.

He had one hundred sixty-five patents over the years, beginning with the image dissector, an improvement over the spinning disc, in 1928.) Television was then refined to such a degree that one could indeed see, in moderately-good detail, what was being shown on the screen. It was this intense competition that resulted in television's accelerated development.

Philo Farnsworth, whose youthful dreams became our reality.

By 1928, a show was being aired from 1:30 to 2:00 on Tuesday, Thursday and Friday afternoons. Television broadcasts at that time was largely experi-

---

*Acronyms for Radio Corporation of America and the National Broadcasting Company. RCA owned NBC at that time.

mental; therefore ukulele strumming was the main fare of that time.

The first televised drama was broadcast over Schenectady's experimental station W2XAD. It was entitled "The Queen's Messenger." Viewers saw the picture on television and heard the dialog on radio. This took place in September, 1928.

By the mid-1930s, performers were instructed to wear black lipstick and blue face paint in order to show up well on the little black-and-white screens. The cameras couldn't handle red yet.

Since very few people had television sets in these very early years, producers didn't worry about advertising or pleasing an audience. It was purely experimental. They strove for artistic excellence.

Radio celebrities were among the first to lend their talents to the small screen in the early 1940s. The successful transition from radio to television was brought about by using many of their radio directors, writers, and producers. Actors from the New York stage also responded to the call of television.

As for Hollywood, well, they looked with disdain at the goings on in the television industry and refused to cooperate at first. They not only feared the competition, but were also afraid that the sketchy lighting and camerawork would harm their stars' careers. Too, who would plunk down money to see a movie if they could see the very same stars for free on the little screen in their own living rooms?

It's just a fad, they hoped.

Television moguls felt otherwise. New York's WOR was a pioneer in television broadcasting, and later Los Angeles set up experimental stations W6XA0 and W6XYZ. In those early years, there were few television sets in that range to receive their signal, but it was a start.

The call letters of the stations indicate various things: the preface letter usually refers to the east or west half of the country, the number is the more specific geographic area, the "X" denotes an experimental station, and the last two letters are assigned by the Federal Communications Commission (FCC) to distinguish it from any other station.

In those years, the news media kept us all aware of the exploration and demonstrated the intricacies of the tubes and magic wiring that would soon change world communication, perhaps as much as the Gutenburg Press had done in the fifteenth century. And, at the New York World's Fair of 1939-40, television broadcasting made its public debut.

This was where the talented producer, Fred Coe, first saw a television set demonstrated. RCA was broadcasting from the fair to the one- to two-hundred television receivers in the broadcasting area. President Franklin Roosevelt's opening of the World's Fair on April 30, 1939, marked the beginning of America's regularly-scheduled programming.

The first commercials were aired that year for Procter and Gamble, Socony, and General Mills during a baseball game.

Then our involvement in WWII took top priority, and television development was put on the back burner while the nation focused on more urgent matters. Once the war was over, however, it was full steam ahead for television.

The public wasn't won over right away. Radio was still the principal form of rapid communication. We had been through a heavy depression

Many people saw a television set for the first time at the 1939-40 World's Fair.

and a critical war. We were serious and careful consumers. Hedonism was not a familiar term.

The television industry would help to change that. Americans had spent many years in sacrifice and hardship. It was time for them to forget the ugliness of war and deprivation and enjoy life again. Transmitters for RCA/NBC, CBS*, and Du Mont networks were atop the Empire State Building in 1946, and they were now ready to show their goods to the public.

William S. Paley was CBS's counterpart to David Sarnoff. Paley had initiated wonderful innovations for CBS radio, and he did the same when it branched out into television. He and network president Frank Stanton built CBS up to become a major presence by recognizing the importance of the sponsor and by developing their news and entertainment departments into powerful entities. Paley had the ability to sense what the public would like in the way of programming.

---

* Acronym for Columbia Broadcasting System

Continuous broadcasting schedules during prime time began in 1948, and the price of television sets was finally affordable. The idea of entertainment in one's own home was more appealing for potential viewers now. *Milton Berle's Texaco Star Theater* began on June 8th of that year, and became television's first hit series — and the show that sold the most television sets.

The musicians' union wanted to wait until television was well developed before setting pay scales for their members. The resulting Petrillo Ban made it necessary, then, to air television shows without the services of union musicians, so drama flourished. Presentations of classic plays were the first dramas aired. Film studios felt so threatened by television drama in 1949, however, that it refused to let NBC air kinescopes of plays to which it owned the rights. This forced TV to use its own writers. Under newcomer Fred Coe's leadership, *The Philco Television Playhouse* became the first show to air on a regular basis the original plays of writers who, until then, were unknown. A large number of these writers would

The star of *Milton Berle's Texaco Star Theater*.

later become legends. Airing on Sunday nights, they had an advantage some other anthologies didn't — they were able to use working Broadway actors because many theatres were dark* on Sunday nights. Those actors welcomed doing these television roles since they were a refreshing change from their routines. Having different drama performed each week by outstanding actors served to make television even more popular. Hollywood had shot itself in the foot.

Among the first family comedies were *The Ruggles*, in which lovable Charlie Ruggles starred as himself, and *(I Remember) Mama*, starring Peggy Wood. Both of these shows debuted in 1949.

In just a few years' time, from 1946 to 1950, the number of commercial television stations grew from seven to almost a hundred. The media was catching on!

---

* When a theatre is said to be "dark," that means no show is being presented in it that day.

Left: The Cast of *The Ruggles*. *Right:* The Cast of *(I Remember) Mama*.

As mentioned earlier, radio supplied much of the personnel and expertise to early television. Some of its most popular radio shows were now coming to TV: those of Kate Smith, Red Skelton, Jack Benny, Burns and Allen, *My Friend Irma*, and *The Life of Riley*. These shows' fans could finally see the faces that went with the very familiar voices.

Now that the war was over, returning soldiers were given benefits that enabled them to get vocational training and new homes. People were becoming more optimistic, feeling that a good future was ensured. The television set was watchable in the late 1940s, but not perfected yet. The screen was small, only ten inches, so many consumers would also purchase a "bubble" device to magnify it. Once a television set had been turned on, it would take a little while for the picture to appear. At the beginning of a show, you would see a test pattern, which was used to adjust the picture. A TV set "had 'rabbit ears,' which basically was an antenna that needed frequent readjusting, as did the 'vertical' and 'horizontal' elements because zigzag lines and 'rolling' were continual problems," says Brooklyn television viewer Emily Peters. There were still some bugs to be worked out of the system, so development continued.

THE RUGGLES

STARRING:
Charlie Ruggles
Irene Tedrow
Judy Nugent
Tom Bernard
Jimmy Hawkins
Margaret Kerry

PREMISE:
The father's vexing problems with his family consisting of a wife, two teenagers, and two pre-teens.

MAMA

STARRING:
Peggy Wood
Juddson Laire
Rosemary Rice
Iris Mann
Dick Van Patten
Robin Morgan
Ruth Gates
Kevin Coughlin

PREMISE:
A warm Norwegian family learning to live in the new world of San Francisco.

The Ed Wynn Show was the first network show to originate in Los Angeles. Debuting in 1949 on CBS, it was in a variety-show format with guest stars and Wynn's delightfully bad jokes, told as only he could. This program was shared with the rest of the country by way of kinescope. At that time, television stations in the west had to air either local shows or fuzzy kinescopes from New York. In this case, the fuzzy kinescopes were sent eastward.

In 1950, Hollywood faced a dilemma: Until then the major motion picture studios owned film theatres throughout the country that exhibited only their own motion pictures. This had been deemed a monopoly by the U.S. government in 1948, and thus they outlawed the practice, cutting the studio's profits considerably. Hollywood was floundering. The studio system was ancient history and players by the hundreds, released from their contracts, were suddenly left without any form of security. Many of them left California en masse, seeking work in New York in the new medium of television. Writers followed.

Burns and Allen

Americans, becoming more acquainted with live television, began purchasing — investing in this new and diverse form of entertainment right in their own homes. Movie attendance as a result suffered dramatically, sending the motion picture industry into frightening foreclosures. At the same time, the familiar faces of filmdom's supporting performers were back entertaining us all on our television sets.

Yes, television was speeding into our lives with strength and guidance from backstage production offices, in the fierce struggles mainly between two new moguls, namely David Sarnoff of NBC and Bill Paley of CBS, their egos plus their know-how talent for show biz competition. In selling their products and TV sets, they were most successful in getting the public's attention.

Blacklisting, too, was crippling Hollywood. Many of their most valuable stars were no longer usable because they were on the House of Un-American Activities list as possible communist sympathizers. (To prevent these people from doing their life's work simply because of suspicions, rather than confirmed facts, was quite un-American, too, but that's a topic for another book.)

At the end of the 1940s, theatre producer and TV pioneer, Worthington Minor, of ABC's *Kraft Television Theatre* and NBC's *Lux Video Theatre*, introduced one-hour dramas and half-hour anthologies, attracting the attention of live television's growing audiences. "The anthology format itself, which demanded a constant supply of actors, writers, directors and producers, and was quite different from the episodic series structure featuring a stable cast, always offered something new to viewers. And since anthology dramas provided plenty of work to go around, many actors got their first starring roles in live dramas, while others gained national exposure that was not possible on the stage or eluded them on the big screen," states Anne Everett in the July 2, 2007, issue of The Museum of Broadcast Communications. Terrific news for us TV thespians!

Almost immediately, directors descended upon New York radio/television stations from eastern university drama departments and stock companies, winter and summer. CBS and Tony Minor invited Fred Coe from Yale, Paul Nickell out of North Carolina, Franklin Schaffner from radio's *March of Time*, Yul Brynner from the New York theatre. Coe moved over to NBC and created *Philco Television Playhouse* at this time. He invited New York-trained Vincent Donehue, Ashville, North Carolina's Arthur Penn, and Delbert Mann, also from Yale. *Kraft Television Theatre*'s Maury Holland and Stanley Quinn were already onboard. All followed by outstanding fellow directors and writers. Golden Age? Absolutely!

The directors couldn't have been happier working with professional actors and the feeling was mutual. We all approached the new live television form of theatre optimistically; though, at first, the absence of an audience and its response was a difficulty. Afterwards, there were responses via family, spouse, friends, neighbors, and stranger recognition. Fans caught us and some sent a note, or, earlier on, the newspapers would deign recognition, giving notice of an up-to-date, electronic theatre.

A unique reception of most live television drama broadcasts was a collective one—of the cast and crew (twenty or twenty-five people combined) during an actual performance, a well-oiled machine dedicated and totally involved in a rehearsed second-to-second, half or full-hour mission. The combined relief and satisfaction of the team, often understated in its quietness, was truly rewarding!

The TV directors were excellent managers.

NBC, CBS, ABC*, and Du Mont** were now the main centers of activity for the industry. Shows were usually originating from New York and Chicago.

---

* Acronym for American Broadcasting Company.

** Allen Du Mont had begun as a television-set developer, then became a television-set manufacturer, and finally progressed to network broadcasting. He was television's first self-made millionaire.

Milton Berle's Tuesday night variety show on NBC had given the world of television the "jump start" it needed. An ever-increasing audience would tune in to see what antics he would create that week. Berle's show included a monolog, comedy sketches, singers, dancers, and other entertainment in a format reminiscent of Vaudeville. There would be occasional times of extreme seriousness, as well. For instance, in one show he and an "up and coming young performer" named Danny Thomas had a dialog, then sang a duet, about patriotism.

In Vaudeville, the same act could be used for years as the performers traveled throughout the country, playing to new audiences weekly. However, on television that same audience could be reached with one evening's program. Vaudeville and similar shows — Milton Berle's and Red Buttons', which at first had been so well received — had swiftly reached a saturation point with the viewers demanding variety. New material was needed constantly.

There were a plethora of film idols appearing on live television now. Formerly highly-paid Hollywood actors — good, solid, supporting actors — were coming to New York in droves. I worked with many in live TV. Hollywood was not doing well.

More bad news for Hollywood: the coaxial cable. This was established in 1951, connecting the east to the west, and broadcasts could now be seen nationwide simultaneously. What is a coaxial cable and how does it work? Engineer Don Trettel explains. He begins by describing the workings of regular lines, such as those used by telephones:

> In general this consisted of two copper wires parallel to each other strung from pole to pole across the country.
>
> When an alternating electric current is sent down a wire it creates an electro-magnetic wave in the surrounding atmosphere, which can be heard near electric transmission lines as radio static. It is why your car AM radio fades out near the electric lines. This electro-magnetic wave serves to remove energy from the original transmission on the wires. So over a given length, the signal fades by a given amount. Additionally, "stray" electro-magnetic waves in the atmosphere can interfere with the original transmission on the ordinary wire, causing noise on the signal. Since a typical electrical signal is transmitted using two wires, the interaction between the electro-magnetic waves on each wire can set up interferences with the signal.
>
> In coaxial cable one wire is encased entirely within the second wire (with an insulator between them). This con-

figuration allows all the electro-magnetic energy to remain within the coaxial cable. Therefore no external electro-magnetic wave is generated, resulting in less energy loss to the signal and less interference. With less loss of energy and less interference, more information (such as required for a video signal) can be transmitted on a given line.

Programming was evolving. In the 1950s, TV westerns and anthology series were the crowd pleasers. Radio was again a major player. It was the daddy of live television drama. Ed Wynn, Fanny Brice, Eddie Cantor, Jack Benny, Alice Faye, Burns & Allen, and Fred Allen presented on television much the same manner as they had in the small radio broadcasting rooms. The smallness worked because the screens, too, were relatively tiny. Like TV today, there were specials — dramas, musicals — and the usual news shows surrounding them.

When Jack Klugman first began working in live television, "I was getting like ten bucks a show, twenty bucks. Then the union came in. If you had over five lines, you got a hundred and a quarter. Under five lines, you got sixty bucks."

Thankfully, unions came onto the scene; actors would earn fair wages. My first live-TV job paid $75 for the half-hour job. This additional income between theatre jobs promised to make life easier. TV wasn't so bad after all.

So much of early television was uncharted territory, which allowed the writers' imaginations free reign. Actors enjoyed the freedom, as well. The producers didn't have large budgets, so they had to be creative. Just what writers and actors loved to do. Consequently, they blossomed.

Neighbors came together to watch their favorite shows. FROM THE COLLECTION OF ONLY CLASSICS

Future superstars were to be found everywhere in New York City when they were between acting jobs. Character actor Albert Salmi and I both used to usher at theaters — he at the Alvin and I at the Astor. I ushered weeknights from 6:00 to 11:30 for nineteen dollars a week. Working nights left my daytime hours open for job searching. I operated the soda fountain, my favorite non-acting job, at Walgreens.

George Peppard supplemented his acting income by working as a motorcycle mechanic and a bank clerk on Wall Street. Robert Cummings served as delivery boy, taxi driver, nighttime switchboard operator, elevator operator, and any other temporary job he could find that would subsidize his dream of becoming a full-time actor someday. He was in good company.

By late 1952, over thirty-three percent of the homes in the United States had a television set. Seven years later, it would be almost eighty-six percent.

Television altered the way Americans lived. They were watching TV shows instead of reading, attending the theater, or listening to the radio. Students were being lured away from their studies by the box. Their social lives were enhanced, however, when neighbors gathered around the set to see their favorite shows.

"We got our first TV, a little black and white in a big cabinet, in 1952," says viewer Ted Pilonero, who was a child then. "The TV picture was always fuzzy and my dad always had to play with the rabbit ear antenna to get a passable picture. It was his exclusive job to adjust the antenna."

Early in 1952, our second baby, Michael, arrived at our new house on Long Island, Hicksville/Levittown. Great kid in most every way except he had colic and remained solidly and loudly awake ALL night, which meant June and I were taking turns, walking him the whole time, for nearly three months. That's when we bought our first TV set. We truly appreciated TV because that's how I made a living. We just didn't have time to watch it. Right now, I am trying to remember what entertained us in those early hours, but we loved it because it quieted Mike down.

Children's programming was exceptional during this time. The shows' hosts treated children with respect. There were Buffalo Bob and Howdy Doody on the east coast, and Cowboy Slim and Skipper Frank on the west coast to present material to children that was both educational and entertaining. Los Angeles' KTLA engineer Klaus Landsberg insisted that family values and good taste be adhered to always, and parents were very grateful. The shows' stars would often make personal appearances, too, that were attended by hundreds of happy kids.

Wally Cox had been such a hit in the *Philco-Goodyear Television Playhouse* episode "The Copper" as a blundering police officer that they gave him a show of his own in 1952 entitled *Mr. Peepers*. He played a teacher of science. Also in the cast were Tony Randall, Marion Lorne, and Patricia Benoit. This show was aired live as a summer replacement, then suddenly dropped for the new fall lineup. The viewers missed this gentle show. Sponsored by Reynolds Metals Company, *Mr. Peepers* was soon brought back as a regular series, due to public demand.

Bishop Fulton Sheen had a very unique show in the 1950s. *Life is Worth Living* was on the Du Mont network from 1952 through 1955. For twenty-seven minutes, he would use a chalkboard as his only visual aid and, in a very relaxed manner, discuss subjects common to the viewers — one subject each show. His topics ranged from Communism to pleasure to the existence of God. Because this program was sponsored by a corporation, rather than the Catholic Church, he structured his talks to be less Catholic than just plain common sense and Christian ethics. Response was enormous. He received about 10,000 letters a week from his show's devoted fans. Bishop Sheen went from this show to the next, entitled *Mission to the World*, which aired on ABC from 1955 through 1957.

Bishop Sheen's format was simple, but effective.

Situation comedies were an American favorite because they were about families or other close units of people, and viewers felt a friendly relationship with them. An individual comedian's style of humor would often be wildly popular at first, but sometimes the audience became saturated with it and began seeking something else. In this case, TV performances on a regular basis were not good for a comedian's career. Red Skelton was an exception to this. The public never seemed to tire of him, and he enjoyed high ratings on a continual basis. He was the favorite comedian of fellow humorist Pat Buttram, who explained why the man appealed to so many people. He said that Skelton's secret could well be the fact that he played a variety of characters and the show was only thirty minutes long, so he didn't overstay his welcome. He said that Skelton was one of the very few comedians who was equally skillful at monologs, skits, and pantomime.

Popular, too, was color broadcasting, which was made possible in 1954. I remember being in a crowded restaurant one evening a couple years later when one of its employees came in and adjusted the knobs on the lone television set mounted on the wall. Suddenly, the diners let out a collective gasp. *The Arthur Murray Party* was being broadcast in full color, and it was beautiful! The ladies' bright, colorful gowns were stunning as their partners twirled them around in a beautiful dance. This was the first time many of us had seen a color telecast.

Color cameras were unable to accept white clothing. It was too intense a hue at the time. Personnel substituted blue instead.

Following the final performance of Mary Martin's hit Broadway musical, *Peter Pan*, the play was adapted for television's *Producers' Showcase* and aired with the same cast (Cyril Ritchard, Kathleen Nolan, Tom Halloran, and Robert Harrington) on March 7, 1955, breaking viewership records. Pat

Weaver, head of NBC, had introduced the concept of TV spectaculars (the 1950s equivalent of today's "specials") but, until *Peter Pan*, they had not been especially popular. This one, however, even outranked *I Love Lucy* — an amazing fete.

Another very successful spectacular was aired on May 30th of that year. It's the only time Humphrey Bogart was ever in a live-television drama. He starred in the *Producers' Showcase* episode entitled "The Petrified Forest" with Lauren Bacall, Henry Fonda, and Jack Klugman. Critics loved it!

Incidentally, the first television I did in Hollywood was with Jack Klugman — an episode of *Treasury Men in Action*. Jack's a non-nonsense man and a tribute to the profession.

Commercials had evolved from being about industries to being about specific products. Live TV was especially advantageous for the Polaroid company. It enabled them to demonstrate in real time how quickly their camera developed pictures.

THE ARTHUR MURRAY PARTY

STARRING:
Arthur Murray
Kathryn Murray
Dancing instructors
Guest stars

PREMISE:
Kathryn was the hostess and Arthur taught the audience how to dance. There would also be singing and an occasional comedy sketch, but mainly graceful dancing.

Mary Martin as Peter Pan

THE GOLDBERGS

STARRING:
*Gertrude Berg
Philip Loeb
Harold J. Stone
Robert H. Harris
Larry Robinson
Tom Taylor*

PREMISE:
A likable Jewish family living in the Bronx. Mother Molly Goldberg did her best to solve the problems of everyone in the neighborhood.

AMOS 'N' ANDY

STARRING:
*Alvin Childress
Spencer Williams
Tim Moore
Johnny Lee
Ernestine Wade
Horace Stewart
Amanda Randolph
Lillian Randolph*

PREMISE:
This show had all black characters, most notable of which was George "Kingfish" Stevens, who lived in Harlem and came up with one get-rich-quick scheme after another, much to the dismay of his wife and mother-in-law.

Gary Moore wasn't the only one who treasured Durwood Kirby (upper right). The Polaroid company did, too!

Announcer-sidekick Durwood Kirby was the perfect pitchman, too. His large, able hands made the camera look smaller and very easy to use. Bloopers were welcome in their commercials, as well. If someone moved and their picture turned out blurry, they could just shoot another. With a regular camera, one wouldn't know the picture was blurry until much later, when the film was developed. By then, it would be too late to take another shot.

Ethnic differences were celebrated in this carefree era, as evidenced by such shows as *The Goldbergs* and *Amos 'n' Andy*. This, many felt, led to understanding and gentle tolerance. (*I Remember) Mama*, too, had an ethnic quality to it as we watched the lives of the Norwegian-American Hansen family unfold. The show was cancelled in 1956, but the show's devoted fans objected, so it was brought back for thirteen more weeks. Appearing regularly as brother Nels, television newcomer Dick Van Patten would go on to have a long and successful career, including the hit television show *Eight is Enough*, and is still going strong today.

The public had loved the drama *One Man's Family* so much on radio that it ran continually longer than any other show in radio history and won a Peabody award for excellence. It was then transferred to television and enjoyed success for a few more years. So real did its characters seem that listeners and viewers alike became emotionally involved with this show.

Like many other genres, soap operas came to the small screen from radio. Their target audience was the bored housewife; and their sponsors were detergent companies. Back then, women employed outside the home were among the jaded villains. (My, how times have changed!)

A number of friends had ventured into the live-television world of the ever-popular daily soap opera. Most had gone from radio into television versions. The American Federation of Television and Radio (AFTRA) union salaries had reached

ONE MAN'S FAMILY

STARRING:
Bert Lytell
Marjorie Gateson
Russell Thorson
Lillian Schaaf
Nancy Franklin
Eva Marie Saint
Frank Thomas, Jr.
Arthur Cassell
Tony Randall

PREMISE:
A San Francisco banker with a philosophic son, marriage-minded daughter, rebellious twins, and a mischievous, but lovable, son.

One Man's Family

a median wage, which, if one had a recurring role in a running soap opera, allowed an actor to make a healthy income. So when I had an offer to play a steady boyfriend on the new *Secret Storm* series, I accepted.

Just as episodic theatre became popular with the new television audiences, eventually the soap operas caught on, many of them going from radio stations to the television studios. Not an easy transition for a radio actor from reading scripts before a microphone in a studio to finding one's way to a makeup room and to wardrobe, then delivering memorized words, rehearsed physical moves — all on complicated sets in and around the cameras and their operators.

Memorization had never before been my problem in theatre, summer stock, or regular TV shows. But, for me, the daily hassle of commuting on the Long Island Railroad with the daily memory work was uncomfortable. Reluctantly, at a convenient time for the series and myself, I left the show and a good group of people, returning to regular television and, eventually, film.

Since that experience, I have had nothing but the greatest respect for all those performers and their photographic memories and talent.

TV soap trivia: The word just before I was cast on *The Secret Storm* was that the title was changed from *The Storm Within* because the producers signed on with a new sponsor — Ex Lax ... Ahh, those ad agencies, those sponsors!

After being blacklisted in Hollywood during the McCarthy era, Jane Wyatt had come to New York and worked on live television for a couple of years. Then came *Father Knows Best*, a much-loved situation comedy about the Anderson family, co-starring Robert Young, Elinor Donahue, Billy Gray, and Lauren Chapin. This show was a wonderful vehicle for Wyatt, but she missed "the electricity of live television," so on hiatus from the series, she would go back to New York and do more live TV.

"Live TV was the most fun of all," says singer-actor Bill Hayes, who, with his wife Susan Seaforth Hayes, spent many years as major characters on the daytime drama *Days of Our Lives*. "Since 1999, we've been lecturing on Crystal Cruises, and one of our lectures is on just that. The response is truly amazing. We show brief clips from kinescopes of some of those early days, and people laugh and then they cry. They cry because suddenly they're transported back to when the whole family was gathered around the tiny, wavy screen. It's very moving."

How actors got on that screen is a story in itself.

THE DEVELOPMENT OF TELEVISION

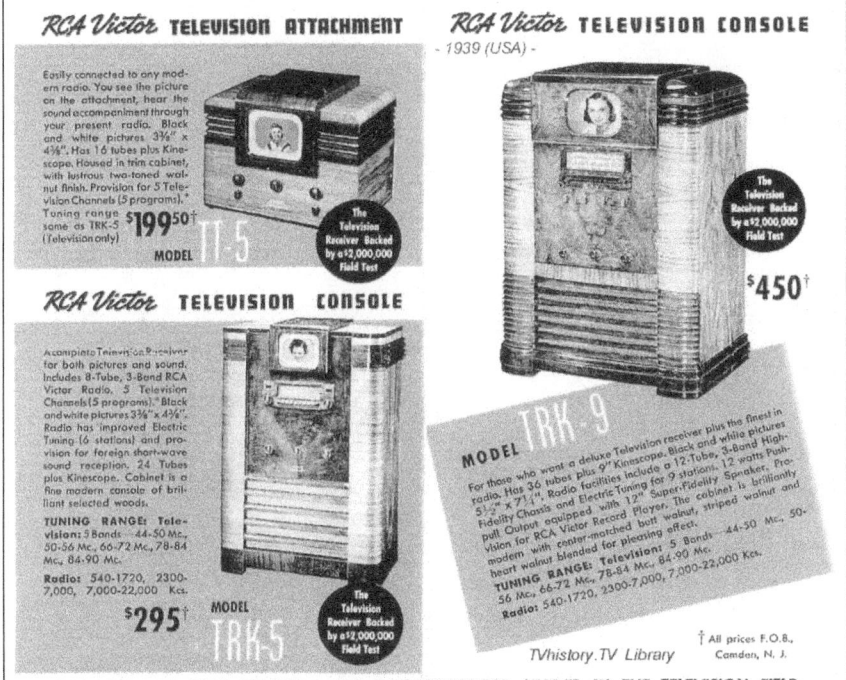

CHAPTER TWO

GETTING THE JOB

How did these performers come to be on our home screens? How did you get your first television jobs, Wright?

After "making the rounds" for four years in and out of summer stock, two years of theatre tours, and three Broadway shows, by then some of the producers and casting people knew me well enough to call me about auditioning or reading for a particular role. For example, by 1950 CBS came up with *Studio One*, a highly successful TV anthology drama program. Their casting office gave me an appointment to read for the director of an upcoming *Studio One* script. I showed up at the appointed time and was given a copy of the play entitled "The Lonely Boy" and told I was to read for a support role, Boy Number Two. I went to the proper page and I studied the scene, observing there were several actors ahead of me. I had time to read the entire script, noticing, much to my surprise and some chagrin, that it was a good story concerning a troubled young man and his family.

Yul Brynner was not only a fine actor, but also an exceptional director.

The role was exactly the same young man I was currently playing on Broadway in *The Bird Cage*, with Melvyn Douglas. The story was different, of course, but, when I was ushered into the room with the director, Yul Brynner, and the assistant, I told him, "I am sorry but, with all due respect, Mr. Brynner, I am interested only in reading for the lead character in this play. And the reason why is that I am currently playing this very character every night at the Coronet Theatre in *The Bird Cage*." Mr. Brynner, a little taken aback, admitted that he knew little of the play, but that he would be interested to hear my reading. Did I need some time to go over it? "No, thank you," I said and, with the assistant director taking the other parts, I read until I was told he'd heard enough and asked if I could return and see him at a time later that day. I returned later, was ushered back into the room where Yul Brynner informed me that he was impressed with my reading, saying "I think you'll be very good in this role." Luckily for me, CBS and *Studio One* must have agreed. The same production was repeated a year later with me and a new cast.

Golden Age employment and managing to stay employed depended on a number of issues. One was keeping attuned to one's urgent profession. A very important move that was a big help for the suddenly-returned WWII veterans, such as myself, was via the GI Bill of Rights that offered college tuition to all returning veterans, including actor veterans via The American Theatre Wing. Yep, that familiar sounding organization literally turned Manhattan into our campus, employing the theatre's top teachers and famed drama coaches into professors. Their offices and studios quickly became our classrooms. In Marian Rich's voice class I studied alongside budding actor Jack Klugman. In actor/teacher Herbert Burghoff's classroom I did scene studies with then actor George Roy Hill and Rod Steiger. With brother veteran Ralph Meeker, I tap danced under the direction of the famous dance man Ernest Carlos. Then under the direction of famed ballet instructor Vitale Folkine, who had long-legged Carleton Carpenter and me trying tours jets upstairs in Carnegie Hall. If there weren't enough veteran actresses to join in the scene study groups, assistance came from volunteer young actresses in current plays — Eileen Heckert, Constance Ford, Maria Karnilova, and others from radio. All this kept the actor in proper shape to compete in a fascinating future of stage, screen and television.

According to actor Albert Salmi's memoirs quoted in his biography, *Spotlights & Shadows*, there was no "cutthroat" issue in the 1940s and 1950s. Rather, actors and actresses helped each other get jobs. If Salmi was turned down for a role, he'd seek out whichever of his actor-friends he felt would be right for it and inform him of the audition. In fact, he once had been *offered* a role but, upon thinking about it, decided he didn't want to do it, so he sent another actor to take his place. That worked out just fine, even though the replacement looked nothing like Salmi.

That turned out great. Let's see how other actors got their start:

Jack Klugman had some good breaks, and that resulted in plenty of work. "I had no agent," he says. "MCA called me and said 'We want to represent you because you're working too much.' They wanted to stop all that because they were afraid I would become an old name."

Klugman played a major role in actor Rance Howard's entry into live television in 1956. Howard had been doing stage work, including a national tour of *Mr. Roberts* with Klugman. Because of the Korean conflict, however, Howard was drafted. "If you wanted to, you could enlist, so I enlisted in the Air Force. Three years, eleven months, eleven days in the Air Force." While he was serving in the military, his fellow actors had been working regularly in this new medium – television. Once discharged from the Air Force, Howard moved back to New York and tried to get into television, too, but with no success. "I didn't have any television experience, and all the casting directors and production people were very wary of an actor with no television experience," he recalls. "So I was making the rounds, trying to get my foot in the door of live television. One day I called up Jack and had lunch with him, and told him my problem – that I didn't have any TV experience and they wouldn't talk with me. Jack had been doing a lot of work for *Kraft Theatre* and he knew the casting director and one of the producers. He said 'I'll see if I can help you.' So Jack called up Marion Dougherty and said 'Hey, I know Rance Howard. He's a good actor. You ought to give him a break.' So they called me for an audition. I went in and auditioned, and I got a part in "Paper Foxhole." That's how I got started. From there, now suddenly I'm an actor with some experience, so the door was opened. Jack Klugman opened the door for me."

Donna Douglas at the beginning of her career, with announcer John Dixon and host Chuck Thompson. FROM THE COLLECTION OF CHUCK THOMPSON

Publicity was, of course, always to an aspiring actor's advantage. It kept his name fresh in people's minds. Chuck Thompson, who worked at WALA-TV in Mobile, Alabama recalls those days in which such publicity was theirs for the taking. "Those were casual times. Almost anyone could walk in and be interviewed on my TV talk show. Ours was the ONLY TV station on the air in a great market. Anyone promoting a record, movie, book, etc., could get air time. Thus I have stories and photos with almost EVERY celebrity of that era…Elvis, Johnny Cash, Dean Martin, Bob Hope, on and on. It was Heaven!" One future celebrity who dropped by his station was beautiful Donna Douglas, of *The Beverly Hillbillies* fame. She was married at the

The cast of *Two Girls Named Smith*

TWO GIRLS NAMED SMITH

STARRING:
*Peggy Ann Garner
Peggy French
Richard Hayes
Joseph Buloff
Marsha Henderson*

PREMISE:
An aspiring model and her cousin, an artist/fashion designer, become roommates in New York City who get into one daffy adventure after another.

time and her name was Dot Bourgeois. She and her husband Roland felt she needed a gimmick to get her career going (talent and drop-dead gorgeous looks weren't enough?), so she was there to celebrate being the champion hot-pepper eater. She was "very agreeable to posing for photos and kidding around," says Thompson. "Had a great sense of humor."

In an interview with Rex Strother, singer Richard Hayes tells how he came to be cast in the 1951 comedy *Two Girls Named Smith*: "Mercury Records is responsible for my meeting my first wife, Peggy Ann Garner, who was already a successful actress, having won a Special Oscar for Outstanding Child Actress in the 1945 'A Tree Grows in Brooklyn.' It's often reported I met and married her because I was her co-star on the show. But the truth is we met before that, at a Mercury Records promotion for one of my records, and we began dating and later we got married.

"'Two Girls' was a live show on ABC on Saturday afternoon. I would drive Peggy to rehearsals and to the broadcast, and then after she would usually drive me to my rehearsals or shows later that night. I was always hanging around the ABC set, waiting for Peggy to get off work. So, I happened to be there the day they fired the guy playing her boyfriend. The director, who knew me from my hanging around, said, 'Do you think you could play her boyfriend?' I figured, sure – being married to her certainly qualified me. So I got the job by being in the right place at someone else's wrong time."

Howard Morris was an important member of the Sid Caesar troupe. When he showed up to audition for *Your Show of Shows*, his diminutive size proved to be a valuable asset. Caesar needed a comical sidekick who was so small that he could pick him up easily, because the script called for this small fellow to jump onto Caesar and cling to him. Howard's trial was a scene in which Caesar lifted him by the lapels. No problem. Up he went, to the glee of all. He was light as a feather! Satisfied that Morris would fill the bill, they hired him.

Carl Reiner, however, was hired for the same show because he was tall. Sid Caesar is a lofty man, but it didn't seem right for his straight man be shorter than he. Thus a call went out for a tall straight man. Director Max Liebman had recently worked with Reiner and felt he would be perfect. How right he was! Reiner's timing was the same as Caesar's, and he had a talent for comedy. He was definitely a team player. Caesar proclaims him to be the best straight man he's ever had. As the years went on, Reiner's son Rob would often be seen on the set, watching the masters work.

The stars of *Your Show of Shows*

Columnist Harold V. Cohen stated that "I've said it before and I'll say it again: Those Sid Caesar-Imogene Coca sketches on *Your Show of Shows* owe a lot to Carl Reiner, their straight man. He's one of the best in the business." It seems a match that was meant to be.

Prolific actor Peter Mark Richman* tells how his wife was cast in a *Playhouse 90* production after he had quit an earlier episode: "I got a call from (director) John Frankenheimer. He wanted me for the same television show three weeks later called 'The Last Man' with Sterling Hayden. I said 'I'd love to come out, but my wife is pregnant and I'm not sure I can leave her.' He said 'Can she act?' I said 'Yes, she's an actress.' He said 'She's hired to play Sterling Hayden's wife.' My wife was seven months pregnant. The story is that Sterling Hayden takes revenge on this town because when he goes to the pharmacy, the pharmacy won't give him pills for his pregnant wife, who is in pain, and she dies."

How ironic! Richman had been a registered pharmacist before becoming an actor.

Ida Lupino and Howard Duff

We've seen actor Steven Marlo in movies and television for four decades, but when he first got to New York, he worked as a waiter, dishwasher, and cab driver. "Every time somebody got into my cab, I used to say, 'Listen, I'm not a cab driver. I'm an actor' just to make myself feel better. Then who should get into my cab one day but Ida Lupino and Howard Duff.

They were in town to do publicity on their series, *Mr. Adams and Eve*. So I turned around and said, 'I'm not a cab driver. I'm an actor.' So Ida Lupino said 'If you ever come out to Hollywood, look us up.' I said 'Okay.' And I thought 'Yeah, sure.' So when I came out to Hollywood to do my first movie, I waited until right after their show was over and called RKO and asked if I could speak to Howard Duff or Ida Lupino. She came on the phone and I

---

* The actor known as Peter Mark Richman today went by the name Mark Richman during the live-TV era. It was later that he adopted Peter as his spirit name.

said 'I'm Steve Marlo.' And she said, 'Well, who are you?' I said, 'I was the cab driver. You asked me to come out if I ever came out to Hollywood.' She said, 'Oh, yeah! Come on out to the studio.' And you know what she did? They wrote a script around me in which I played a prize fighter! They win me in a card game. Just because I said 'I'm not a cab driver. I'm an actor'."

Sometimes, it was family ties that got an actor a job. That might have been

Betty Furness

Betsy Palmer

the case in the March 8, 1953 episode of *Robert Montgomery Presents* entitled "The Burtons." Starring in that show were three members of the same family — Gene and Kathleen Lockhart, and their daughter June. Many of us Baby Boomers thought June's career began with *Lassie*, but, in reality, she was a well-known supporting actress long before then.

Betty Furness was a popular film actress of the 1930s and 1940s, but hadn't had a job in quite a while when her agent called in 1949 to offer her a one-time commercial spot on *Westinghouse Studio One*. She happily accepted. Little did she know that the job would be the beginning of a very long and successful on-screen sales career.

Actress Betsy Palmer was back from a winter stock job when she dropped by to say hello to the typing pool at WGM, where she used to type scripts to earn her way through school. Her former boss came up to her and asked if she'd like to do a television show. She quickly agreed, but knew very little about TV since she knew no one who had a set. There was no money in it, but she took the job for the experience. "We did this live show every day during the week in the afternoon and I would just jabber with him, just off the cuff, no script or anything, and I would describe what the (models) were wearing. They were walking around in lingerie." Her next job was similar to this, but the sponsor was Amling's Flower Land and, thus, the topic of conversation

Wright King, 1946 — making the rounds. "This is how I dressed every day I lived in New York and made my rounds — ALWAYS a tie."

would be flowers and plants. "Stuff I knew absolutely nothing about." From that, she went to live commercials for a Chicago soap opera. Her partner in that job was future game-show host/newsman Hugh Downs, who was under contract to NBC.

From the time my fearless writing partner, Sandra Grabman, talked of sharing this book, up comes actress Betsy Palmer. Sandra earlier on asked me if I knew Miss Palmer. I sure do know this lady! Betsy is a living ray of sunshine. I can't recall the name of one of her earlier morning television appearances, in maybe 1952, but she'd show up on her channel and brighten my day. Her spirit pervades the air from the game shows through her more serious thespian moments. All the way to the happy surprise in Panama City, Florida, when she appeared on the musical stage in the road company of Lerner and Lowe's *GiGi*.

Another time, Betsy Palmer had walked into the small apartment of actor Frank Sutton and his wife Toby. He would someday be a major player in *Gomer Pyle, USMC*, but back then he was struggling just like so many others. "Frank, in those days, couldn't get arrested," she recalls. "In the small living room, over in the corner was a man sitting facing the door with three other guys, talking. He saw me come in, and I heard him say, 'Well, she'd be perfect,' and he motioned for me to come over. He said, 'Are you an actress?' I said — I'd just come to New York and didn't know what this was all about — 'Yes!' He said, 'Monday, go see so-and-so at this agency. Tell them that I sent you.' So Monday, I went to see this man. He said 'Do you have a southern accent?' I said, "I sho' 'nough do, honey.' And I did a soap opera for three or four months."

Betsy might be most well known to fans of the 1950s and 1960s for her work on panel-style game shows. Peter Arnell, an employee of the Goodson-Todman office, was one of the men at the Suttons' apartment that day. He and Betsy bumped into each other some time later as she was going to a job interview for a hostess position at Schrafft's restaurant. He talked her into working on a game show he had written, which opened up a whole new career for her.

Okay, now the job is gotten. What's next?

CHAPTER THREE

ON THE JOB

Wright, what was it like the first day?
Speaking as an actor, mainly in episodic live television. The first day of rehearsal took place generally in a rented rehearsal hall, or rarely on the stage of a vacant theatre. The director met with the entire cast at a table set by the stage manager with ancient folding chairs for each actor. The stage manager in turn began the reading by announcing the acts, as well as the script's printed directions. All acts were read by the cast in proper order with the director making few, if any, comments. A first reading is an awkward ritual, but a necessary exercise of collective bargaining. This system comes directly from professional theatre.

After the first reading came the blocking -- direction of the actors' physical moves throughout the scenes, where they sit, stand or walk. For this, the stage manager, prior to the rehearsal, according to the playwright's direction, chalk and tape measure in hand, draw lines to indicate the actual size and space, windows, doors of each particular scene. Three of four folding chairs become a sofa, one a chair table, etc., exactly the size of the actual setting on the studio floor.

A majority of the performers involved in television at this time had been theatre oriented. Rehearsal is crucial, and there is a lot of it. That's probably why this was later called "The Golden Era of Television" — because, after such extensive rehearsal, they were able to present a quality product.

You know that they say the three most important things in real estate are "location, location, and location"? That could be said about theatre, as well — of utmost importance is "rehearsal, rehearsal, and rehearsal."

Central to the rehearsal is the time designated to the episode. The half hour shows (*Danger*, etc.) were by the big studios allotted five days rehearsal, including the actual shooting date, and the hour programs (*Philco*, etc.) were rehearsed and performed in a seven-day period. Summer stock performances were allowed the same weekly rehearsals, which is why when television entered the scene, it was accurately termed "Summer stock in an iron lung."

Rehearsal was crucial. Over the next few days, with a competent director, the play improved daily. Most times the play would take on new dimensions

during this time of preparation and find the script in proper shape for the actual performance.

The exceptions to the above rehearsal and schedules varied in different ways. For example, when, with David Niven, the four of us actors performed "Journey's End", a Christmas Eve sketch, on Ed Sullivan's *Toast of the Town*, we rehearsed in one of the Mallon studios in a three-day session. The final day was, as I recall, in a small room adjacent to a waiting "green room", where I noticed an attractive young lady perched solemnly on a high stool, awaiting her time to perform. Ed called out her name, announcing "talented new singer", the solemn lady put on her best smile and on pranced Rosemary Clooney, singing the hell out of "Ain't She Sweet?"

In contrast with today's practices, the writers of dramatic shows generally had the freedom to come and go on the set, and were available to make whatever last-minute changes were necessary.

Ed Sullivan

Comedian Sid Caesar's shows had a unique routine: Monday a.m. — The writers (which often included such talent folk as Neil and Danny Simon, Woody Allen, Dick Cavett, etc.) began getting ideas, then built on it and wrote the script. Wednesday night - The script was completed. Thursday — The show was on its feet. Friday — Technical rehearsal. Saturday — Rehearse morning and afternoon, then air live that evening.

It was in 1954 that Wright co-starred with Dorothy Gish in the *Philco Television Playhouse* episode entitled "The Shadow of Willie Greer," written by Horton Foote and directed by Vincent J. Donehue. There was one scene that was especially impressive. As critic Hift wrote, "Dorothy Gish as the grandmother provided a busy and believable character sketch. Her scene in which she dictated a letter to her grandson (King) was outstanding." This was a complex role for Wright. Quoting Hift again, "His taciturn character contrasted oddly with that of the old man (grandfather, played by William Hansen) who offers him his love and asks his forgiveness." What do you remember about this show, Wright?

Dorothy Gish was a first-class actress and a delight to work with. I believe that this Horton Foote script was Ms. Gish's initial role on live television and it didn't faze her for a minute. Her sister Lillian Gish was with her after one of the rehearsals; she'd worked on *The Philco Theatre*, also in a Horton Foote play. BOTH Gish sisters! You don't get any better than that. They were radiant, lovely women.

Dorothy Gish and Wright King in "The Shadow of Willie Greer" FROM THE COLLECTION OF WRIGHT KING

Daytime television "soaps" allowed the least amount of rehearsal time because they were broadcast five days a week. The cast of *The Guiding Light*, for example, first read the script the day before it was to be aired. It was blocked and rehearsed a couple times in the morning, the day of the broadcast, then aired live. "Everybody's keyed up," says actress Judy Robinson, who played Robin Lang Fletcher on the show, "all the staff people — the camera people, the grips, and all. They had this kind of energy. It was so exciting. You're totally focused. You know you can't redo it. You focus on the moment."

Actress Helen Wagner has been with *As the World Turns* for over fifty years. She and her cast mates were scheduled to be at the studio at 7:30 a.m. to prepare for the half-hour show, which aired at 1:30 p.m. Those who then had no scenes in the next day's show could go home when it was over at 2:00. The others began rehearsing again at 2:30. If they wanted to take time off to do another project, such as a Broadway play, they would be written out for a while, then the story line might allow for them to return when that project was over.

For panel game shows, there was no rehearsal. The members of the panel just had to be at the studio an hour before the broadcast.

Comedian Jackie Gleason had an exceptional memory, having his lines already memorized after reading the script once, so his preparation time was shortened. Fortunately, when it came to live shows, he was a great ad libber, as well. Rehearsals for his "Honeymooners" sketches took place in the star's hotel apartment.

The comedy *Two Girls Named Smith* aired at noon on Saturday. Therefore, stars Peggy French and Peggy Ann Garner, along with their on-screen neighbors, had to be on the set for final rehearsals that morning at 7:30. They had it easy. The stage crew had been there since 10:30 the night before, dismantling the *Pulitzer Prize Playhouse* set and setting theirs up, and technicians began coming in at 3:00 a.m.

Okay, Wright, you're at the rehearsal hall and into rehearsals. What's next?

That's a good question, Sandra…or is it?

Director Sidney Lumet, a bold pioneer of The Golden Age. Among his successes was CBS's weekly half-hour episode of *Danger*. Always an exciting and satisfying experience. I was fortunate to have done a number of *Dangers* and was happy to be cast as a semi-pro baseball player in this upcoming episode. We lived on Long Island at the time. Working out with my son and neighbors on Little League ball playing, I was glad I could answer in the positive when Sidney inquired if I could pitch. We rehearsed the required three or four days, and then went for the last day and a half in the actual set in the CBS studio. Of course, there was no regular baseball diamond — just a mock-up area pitcher's mound. "Wright," came my name on the loudspeaker from Sidney, followed by Sidney's "would you get on the pitcher's mound in front of the camera and give me a wind-up and a couple of throws? I want to see what you look like on the screen in here," he informed. "Sure thing," I answered, stepping up to the mound, taking a pause before a carefully thought-out windup, and followed through with a serious curve ball, then stopped, awaiting further direction. There ensued a long pause before Sidney asked if I could repeat my windup and pitch. "Can do," I reassured. Taking extra care to repeat my last throw, I wound up and threw the pitch. A wait, and then a longer pause. I was surprised at seeing Sidney emerge from the control room, walking directly up to me, stopping, looking straight into my eyes, and, in a low, serious voice, announcing, "You're kidding." Shattered…in a second I got it. "Oh, my God," I thought. "Sidney's a New Yorker…The Dodgers, the Yankees! Ohhhh! He's a big baseball fan!!!" "I'm sorry, Sidney…" He, his magic and talent, I'm certain, made it a competent show. It took a while before I worked with him again.

Usually the cast of an upcoming play met at a specific broadcasting sound stage the day before the actual broadcast. They were met generally by the assistant director and guided through the various sets. He also acquainted them with the hair-dressing, makeup, and wardrobe people, and showed them their dressing and rest rooms. Afterward, the director started rehearsals and restaged scenes, if necessary. A newcomer-actor would find it difficult to ignore the chaos consisting of lights, cameras,

booms, dollies, and the jungle of cables obscuring the floor, plus a permanent crew of nineteen members.

Sometimes, the sound stage had dimensions different than what they had considered during rehearsal. That's when the restaging was needed so that the timing would be right and things would go smoothly.

If one is accustomed to acting on stage, he must tone down his gestures for television, which is much more intimate. A simple wink or pursed lips spoke volumes on television, whereas they would be unnoticed on stage.

Actor Jack Klugman had a way around this. "I would say 'Move the camera back. Don't do such a close-up.' And the guys would do it." When the camera is farther away, those grander stage-like gestures aren't as overwhelming as they would be in a close-up.

Sid Caesar likens the broadcast of each show to opening night on Broadway, except his material was much newer (only six days old!) and his audience was about 40,000 times larger. They performed before a live audience, who would watch most of the show on the large screen atop the stage on the proscenium. That way, they could see the same close-ups the viewers at home were seeing. To indicate the passage of time, they would show a minute or hour hand rapidly circling the clock, or flip pages of a calendar. If an exterior shot were needed, a camera would be focused on a photograph of the scene. They used no cue cards or teleprompters on this show because Caesar felt they would only get in the way of acting.

In live television dramas, and often comedies as well, there were several stage sets lined up in a row. Sometimes, the scene in the one the actors just left would be changed, just in the nick of time for them to re-enter it. It was necessary in this and all live shows with multiple sets for the writer to give an actor time to get from one set to another and to make a costume change, when necessary. A well-placed commercial would give him about seventy seconds to change. If there were none at that time, then he usually wouldn't be the first character to appear in the next scene. That gave him a few precious moments. Sometimes, however, there *was* no time. In such a case, a dresser would be changing the actor's trousers and shoes as the camera was on his face. Teamwork was so necessary back then. The actors and the crew worked very closely together to make these shows progress as smoothly as possible.

Because of the smallness of some of the studios, there were usually only two or three sets to work with. They weren't necessarily set up in the order in which they were to be used, either. Thus, added to the challenge of going from one to the other was ducking cameras and jumping over the ever-present cables covering the floor. The actor dashing to the next set was frequently out of breath when he got there.

What appealed most to actor Rod Steiger about live television was that it was very much like repertory theatre. Actors of his ilk were cast in television dramas with regularity, so in a few weeks' time, he would have played several very different characters. Just the thing to increase a young actor's versatility, making him more employable.

Peter Mark Richman agrees. Live television was a great training ground for actors. If one can perform well on television live, he can perform well anywhere.

Left: Rod Steiger. *Right:* Albert Salmi, Claire Kirby, and Rod Steiger FROM THE COLLECTION OF CLAIRE KIRBY HOOTON

"It was a high-pressure time," says Claire Kirby Hooton*, who prefers the more relaxed atmosphere of working on film or tape.

Indeed, the tension was incredible and performers were known to suffer from it. According to *TV Digest* in 1953, "Dean Martin and Jerry Lewis admit that the strain of one television show is equal to that of two performances an evening on a night club floor, two weeks running."

Live television differed from stage work in a way because you had only one chance to get it right. Once it aired, that was it. The strain was too much for some, who developed bleeding ulcers or had heart attacks.

As Joan Davis told *TV Digest*, "I was so tired one day, I started to cry, as women sometimes do, from nervous exhaustion. Then I thought, 'My eyes. My face!' It'll hold up production, at $400 an hour, if I do. So I held back the tears. In television, you don't have time to be a woman." That's probably

---

* Claire went by the name Claire Kirby during the live-TV era. She is now going by her married name of Claire Hooton.

especially true for the star of the show, as Miss Davis was.

Betsy Palmer managed to be very much a woman in spite of live television's demands. She delighted in it, in fact. "When you're doing live television, it's like doing the theatre," she says. "That's what was exciting about it. The red light would go on on the camera, and sink or swim. You had to survive for that hour, or half hour, or whatever it was. It was exciting, very exciting. I loved it!"

Top Left: Don Grady. *Top Right:* Kathy Garver. *Bottom Right:* Wright King in *Matinee Theatre*, directed by Alan Buchanz. May, 1956

Many felt that this type of acting was not only exciting, but also emotionally satisfying for an actor, just as stage plays were. There was a team feeling, too. The cast and crew were respectful of one another.

Did child actors in live TV receive respect, too? Yes, says Don Grady, who began acting at age thirteen. "But no monkey business was tolerated."

Kathy Garver, later of *Family Affair* fame, agrees. A child of the 1950s, she remembers loving it on the set of *Climax* and *Matinee Theatre*. Children were treated well there.

I believe *Matinee Theatre* was the very last running live television program. It seems to have begun in New York and migrated to California, located then near the famous Hollywood and Vine intersection.

Such flexibility was an asset. The move west, however, changed the nature of television and acting became a lot different.

Many actors remember most the pressure of working live, but Steven Marlo has a different point of view. "For live TV, at least you have a chance to really rehearse a lot. Live TV, you're got to rehearse it. There wasn't as much pressure on live TV as it is in filmed TV. Not for me, it wasn't. I always had a tough time memorizing lines because it didn't come easy for me, so I had to work at memorizing the script. For taped TV, you come in and you shoot. You rehearse maybe a take or two, then boom, you shoot it. It's Boom! Boom! Boom! What was happening mostly on filmed TV, you've got a bunch of these young directors. There's a certain budget, and you have to do it then and there, and go to the next scenes. Whereas on live TV, you had more mature directors and more time to rehearse. It was more like theatre."

The directors, while perhaps more mature, were not always of advanced years. George Roy Hill (born in 1921), Delbert Mann (1920), Franklin Schaffner (1920), Paul Nickell (1915), Ted Post (1918), Jeffrey Hayden (1926), Paul Bogart (1919), John Frankenheimer (1930), and Arthur Penn (1922) seem to have dominated the airways during that era.

Buzz Kulik was one of the few live television directors originating in Hollywood. He was a solid reminder of a way of life left behind in New York TV and was yet another director that I enjoyed working with.

Kulik was a frequent director for *Lux Video Theatre*, which moved to Hollywood in 1953. *Climax* and *Playhouse 90* benefited from his talents, as well.

Oftentimes in these very early years, cameras for one show would be borrowed from another show across town. This was done for the 1949 show *The Admiral Broadway Revue*, which was broadcast by two networks, NBC and Du Mont. As Sid Caesar explained in his book *Caesar's Hours*, "At the time, the coaxial cable went only as far as Chicago. West of that, shows were recorded on kinescopes and rebroadcast a week later." Fortunately, some of those kinescopes survive to this day. Most, though, appear to have been discarded. If a show was to be aired again, they did not always use the kinescope. Often, they would simply perform it a second time.

As wonderful a team as Caesar and Imogene Coca were, one would think they spent a lot of off-camera time together, right? Not so. They interacted very little off-stage. Perhaps that's what kept their work so fresh — no peripheral emotional baggage. That seemed to be the norm for many working relationships back then.

Even though much of live television was hit or miss, there *were* some rules of good taste that were strictly observed. The guidelines for many shows were as follows: Sex and religion were off limits. Politicians could be spoofed in general, but no specific politician would be portrayed. The same with corporations. Foul language was off limits and, of course, they were never to demean a sponsor. Rules such as these could be stifling for some, but they just served to make show-biz folk even more creative.

Comedy, Caesar feels, is best done live — straight through, from beginning to end with no break. It has a rhythm that gives it life.

The long-running series *Studio One* had its first hit on March 6, 1949. It was a modern version of "Julius Caesar," starring Philip Bourneuf, Robert

Sid Caesar and Imogene Coca

Keith, and William Post, Jr. in modern-day garb. One of *Playhouse 90*'s biggest hits was Rod Serling's "Requiem for a Heavyweight," starring Jack Palance, Keenan Wynn, Ed Wynn (playing against type in a serious role), and Kim Hunter. Says Palance researcher Stone Wallace, "The *New York Times* review of the show was delayed from its usual placement in the morning edition because critic Jack Gould was so enthusiastic over the program that he needed more time to write his review."

I co-starred in a *Kraft Television Theatre* presentation once with Rod Steiger in "The Man Most Likely," a play modeled along the lines of "Death of a Salesman." The story was about two New York Jewish brothers, with Steiger as the Biff-type older son and me as his younger brother. We had that fine director, Maury Holland, and the week of rehearsals went smoothly. It was an exciting play and a promising adventure. As with all the Kraft broadcasts, it was a one-time presentation. We took our places before the camera, the red camera lights put us in the eyes of millions of viewers, and Rod proceeded to cry! He cried through the entire hour, ignoring all

of the rehearsal to the contrary. **Whether it made the story better or not, I don't know, but it sure puzzled the rest of the cast. Rod was an enigma.**

Tears came easily to Rod Steiger, but another director came along and taught him that it's oftentimes more effective to control one's emotions:

One of the most important dramas of 1953, perhaps of the whole era, was a hurriedly-written fill-in. *The Philco Television Playhouse* was originally to present a different story, but the script had been terrible, so they asked Paddy Chayefsky, who had already proven himself a very talented author, to finish a script he was in the midst of writing so they could perform it. "Marty" was the result. It was a simple story — a plain butcher, who had been rejected by women again and again, but was nevertheless nagged by his mother to get married, meeting a young lady who had been deserted by her date because of her homeliness. His heart goes out to her but she, having been hurt once too often, is afraid to trust him at first. His sincerity and basic goodness eventually win her over. This was one of the most influential dramas ever. In Harold V. Cohen's regular *TV Digest* column, he lobbied for a repeat of this performance, stating, "Chayefsky's study of a couple of little people was a touching thing full of tenderness and pathos, and Rod Steiger and Nancy Marchand gave the kind of performances that would be Oscar candidates if they had been played in the movies."

As mentioned earlier, rehearsals took place all over New York in rented halls before studios were made large enough for such things. Recalling their preparation for "Marty," Betsy Palmer, who played Marty's cousin, says, "There was a Scandinavian restaurant that was down below (the rehearsal hall). This was upstairs and it was a hall that I bet (director) Del Mann picked out and, when he found it, said 'This is perfect,' because it was for men and women to meet. A dance place. The girls would stand on one side of the hall and the guys would be on the other side. It was one of those clubs, a friendship club, I think it was called. I remember going into the girls' bathroom and there would be signs on the wall, 'Remember men have feelings too, girls,' not to be rude to them. And it really worked because it was the right space to be in for this particular show. And, of course, Nancy Marchand has always been a great actress.

"I remember learning a big lesson from dear Del Mann, because he said to Rod (who kept crying during rehearsal because he felt so sorry for his character), 'Will you stop with the tears? If you cry for yourself, your audience will never cry for you.' He was absolutely right. You can't cry for yourself because then the audience pulls away." Steiger gave it a mighty effort, and the result was exactly as Mann had hoped. "It was the best-controlled performance he has ever given in his life," he said.

Since cameras weren't able to move around easily during a scene, the actors would do the close-up nearer to the camera, like in Marty's dance scene. When Rod's character was talking, he'd be positioned so the camera would see his face. Then they would turn so Nancy's character could be seen as she

Rod Steiger and Nancy Marchand in dance scene of "Marty" PHOTOFEST

spoke. They had very little room for the dance floor because the studio was cluttered with sets, so there was space for only one camera.

"Marty" was a very intense television drama. When they later made it into a movie, however, they had to tone it down because it was twice as long. An audience can take only so much intensity.

According to *The Box*, authored by Jeff Kisseloff, Lee J. Cobb suffered a heart attack during the airing of the 1955 *Producers' Showcase* episode entitled "Darkness at Noon," but stayed in character and finished the story. Once the show was over, he then sought the medical care he needed. That's dedication!

A goodly number of the live television critics and reporters proclaimed that live television was often as professional as a Broadway play. The directors and writers were outstanding, as were the actors. E. G. Marshall, Harry Townes, Nancy Marchand, as well as many others, were recognized television talents for as many as three decades.

Indeed, live television was just loaded with very, very talented people. It gave them the freedom to create, and exposure that advanced their careers greatly.

Prop personnel and people in charge of scenery were quite professional, as well. KTLA in Los Angeles had a program called *Frosty Frolics*, in which the performers were ice skaters. The sets were made of thin cardboard, but Sherman Laudermilk brilliantly made them appear real to the home viewer. Stagehands had to be adept at skating in order to put scenery and props in place in a timely manner on this show.

Versatile Merv Griffin, who would later become a game-show host, actor, producer, director, and music composer, was a regular on *The CBS Morning Show* for a while. The sponsor for this show was American Airlines, who served the stars breakfast on the air each morning. The first show of the day was fine, but they had to perform the show again at 9:00 for the West Coast. Still, he had to look like he was enjoying eating that very same breakfast again. Not easy to do on a full stomach. (In this case, the later development of videotape was a godsend.)

Merv Griffin

Assigned as a summer replacement for Eddie Cantor, actor Alan Young's show, too, had to be performed twice each time — 8:00 p.m. for the rest of the country, and 11:00 p.m. for the West Coast. There was audience aplenty for the earlier show, but the seats often had to be filled by their agents' family members for the late one.

Andy Griffith's 1955 appearance on *The U.S. Steel Hour* was a break from that show's usual fare. Their plays were almost always dramatic and quite serious, but, this time, it was a comedy entitled "No Time For Sergeants." How ironic it was that the future sheriff of Mayberry played a Gomer Pyle-sort of character in this play! It worked, though. It would turn out to be a hit.

Composer/musical director Irving Robbin recalls working with young actors for the show *Tales of Tomorrow*, which was a science-fiction anthology show. "Our actors were generally in the earliest stages of their careers — Leslie Nielsen is a good example of that. And Paul Newman," he says. "James Dean did one for us, right out of The Actor's Studio. He felt that TV acting should be totally free and that he could go anywhere on the floor and the cameras should follow him, no matter what he did. He got a good lecture on hitting marks and moving on the right dialogue lines. I guess it prepared him for Hollywood."

Prior to the first dress rehearsal, we'd all sit at a long table and read through the revised script. Rewrites may or may not have been done. We did a lot of cutting, much to the chagrin of the writers, who would sit there and stew.

In the viewer's home, the aerial had been installed on the roof and the rabbit ears had been adjusted atop the large television console. The family was seated and waiting for the set to warm up so they could be entertained.

At that moment, the actors at the studio had landed their parts, learned their lines, and were well rehearsed. They were on their marks, ready for the floor manager to give them their cue to begin. They were ready to boogie.

CHAPTER FOUR

AIR TIME!

Okay, Wright, it's now zero hour. What was it like on the set?

Tensions were high, gaining momentum as the moment of the broadcast drew near. There was an emotional electricity in the air. Our stomachs did flip-flops before, and now we were on the air. The camera was staring at you and its red lights were on, which meant it was broadcasting. The wonderful thing about this was that the actor was on his own. A bittersweet responsibility. Immediately, you would see a busy young man, the floor manager, rushing about on the sound stage, complete with headset attached to a long electric line. He was involved in facilitating communication between the control room and everyone on the floor. At one point, probably near the very end of the show because of timing mishaps, he would crouch just in front of the final camera but out of sight of the viewing audience (while in full sight of the final players), holding both hands before him a slight distance apart and slowly bringing them together, indicating "Slow it down." To hasten our delivery, he would signal by rolling his hands palm over palm. These signals were rarely used, however, because we had established the perfect timing during prior rehearsals, ending up pretty much on the head.

The audience saw just the actors, but actually there were about nineteen other people on the floor. We were all working together as a close team to bring you the best show possible. It was a very special time of complete cooperation and the result was true art.

Says Rance Howard, "It's close to [the feeling of] a Broadway opening. When they say 'One minute until air time' and counting down, that's just about like the curtain opening on a Broadway play. You get such a rush of adrenalin. It's really, really exhilarating."

The hours were long on the day of a live television show's broadcast. The performers of *The Steve Allen Show* were required to be at the studio by 7:00 Sunday morning for a show that aired at 8:00 p.m.

Claire Kirby was to play the lead in a show, but woke up with nerve-induced blemishes on her face the morning of the broadcast. Makeup could not sufficiently cover them, either. "So they turned me away from the camera, with my back to the camera."

Speaking of her 1955 *Hallmark Hall of Fame* episode about John Paul Jones, Gloria Jean says "It was scary, but a lot of fun."

Nervousness manifested itself in different ways for different people. When cast as the title character in *You Are There*'s "The Death of Cleopatra," Kim Stanley almost gave the floor manager a heart attack when, after the "Five minutes to air, company onstage" announcement, she ran back to the dressing room and redid her makeup.

"It was terribly challenging and the pressure was enormous," added Peter Mark Richman. "Working up to that time to get on the air was absolutely nerve wracking. You know that you are suddenly confronting 20 million people and there's no going back. Whatever you do is permanent. There're no retakes." In remembering one particular show, Richman says, "I had the part of a cop with a show in which I was coming in to investigate an old lady who was causing some problems in the neighborhood. She seemed to be going out of her mind, and I didn't come in until the second act. That was about fifteen minutes into the show. I want to tell you that was one of the most nerve-wracking experiences of my life…It was just debilitating. After you get started, it's okay, but just waiting on live television was just awful for an actor."

Peter Mark Richman and actress Peggy Ann Garner, with whom he worked on both stage and television FROM THE COLLECTION OF PETER MARK RICHMAN

Still speaking of this program, Richman continues, "It was a very important show for me because I remember specifically that I had these big close-ups, watching the woman when I investigated the house and was talking to them. I was a pleasant guy just trying to study the situation, and I was looking at this lady, with questioning looks on my face. It helped me get a lot of shows after that…star billing in live shows."

When there were musical interludes, they usually took place right there in the studio and, thus, were heard by the actors. Usually, there were at least three cameras on the set. The close-ups were done by the cameras on each side (which had to be angled in such a way that they wouldn't be in the picture shot by the camera on the other side), and the full view came from the center camera.

Everything that was happening on the show went to the control room, which looked much like a radio broadcasting booth, except for a large monitor screen whereon were about four monitors, one for each camera out there on the floor. Each screen was no larger than 14 x 16 inches and had a number on it that would coincide with the number of the live camera whose scene it was displaying. On the counter before the director was a keyboard with keys that matched the cameras. On a command from the director, a union producer sitting next to the director had edited the entire production as it was being aired. Directing a big-time TV production was always a hairline balancing act. Kinescopes, taking movies of the productions off the television screen, were mostly for internal use and seen only in producers' screening rooms.

What the studio audience notices, but the television viewer probably doesn't, is that when two actors are in a close-up together, they have to be really close to each other. Sometimes, that's fine. Other times, well, let's just say an actor hoped his cast mate did not have garlic for lunch.

Live television was difficult for the actors and the directors, but the makeup artists' job was no picnic either. Take, for instance, *The Philco Television Playhouse* episode "Crown of Shadows." This was the makeup artist's ultimate challenge. The Carlotta character had to age and youthen twice during the show, back and forth in time.

Here's another test of technical know-how: The *Producer's Showcase* episode "Darkness at Noon," starring Lee J. Cobb, had to alternate for a while between Cobb's being in a jail cell and his flashbacks to earlier times. This was accomplished with a jail set with only two walls. The camera to one side would show Cobb with the cell as background, then the camera on the other side would be at the opposite angle, showing him with a different background. He remained in the same position, but appeared to be in two different places! Ingenious!

When everything was happening in the same area, it was relatively easy to be coordinated. Imagine what it was like for Paul Nickell, director of *Ford Star Jubilee* episode "A Bell For Adano," in which the play was acted in one studio, the commercials took place in the studio beside it, and the David Rose Orchestra was providing its music from the studio across the hall! Did we mention that space was frequently a problem in New York City?

Probably the worst live-TV experience Merv Griffin ever had took place in 1957 on the show *Going Places*, which he was hosting. It was the second show of the series and, right before air time, he got a call from his sister Barbara. Their beloved father had suddenly died, at age fifty-five, of a massive heart attack. Within minutes, he was on the air and had to appear carefree. He was jovial on the outside, but crying on the inside, something only a very gifted actor can do.

Outdoor scenes in westerns were sometimes a challenge to do convincingly. Sometimes an airplane overhead would threaten to take the viewer away from the old west and return his thoughts to the present day. Suspension of disbelief was necessary at such times. Microphones were oftentimes hidden on the hitching posts or in trees, so the bad guys had to do their dastardly business near those points.

After a live show was aired, the actors were sometimes invited to go back to see it on kinescope a couple days later, but Betsy Palmer wouldn't take them up on it. "It was always very grainy and, of course, black and white," she said. "And the lighting. They didn't do the lighting (well) in those days."

Kinescope images were notoriously rough, crude, and badly lit; but it was the only option of preserving our work available to us at the time.

Wright King featured in *Studio One*'s "Paris Feeling," directed by Franklin Schaffner in 1951

Once the last moments of the final scene were ended and the credits rolling, we would have an overwhelming feeling of "Thank God it's over!" The build-up of tension was gone. But strangely, we'd still be looking forward to the next one.

Backing up a little about "the show being over" — well, not over for everyone. Not for popular young motion picture starlet, Ann Gillis. I had followed her successful career over the years and was happily surprised to find that she'd been cast as my true love in CBS *Studio One*'s "The Paris Feeling." It was a big success for us both. Not long ago, we met at a film festival in Memphis. She was the same girl in many ways and it was a warm meeting until, sadly, she stated, "We did the show and that was it. It was all over." Strange. On finishing a movie script in Hollywood, there's almost always a "wrap party," a goodbye get-together. Not so then in New York in live TV. Much like in the radio days before, the cast just departed with "Nice working with you" or "See ya later."

Once the show was over and those involved left the studio, they would then get an unofficial critique of the show.

The following morning after a television appearance, commuting on the Long Island train back to New York, I sat beside a man who, studying me, said, "You on television last night?" Turning, I said, "Yeah, a *Danger*."

He said "Can I tell you something?" I replied, "Sure, go ahead." " ...Not quite so much..." he advised.

The only problem was — once the public learned of an exceptionally wonderful show, it was too late. It was already over. They could only hope that the same show would be presented again sometime with the same actors and director, but that did not happen very often.

Memories

Peter Mark Richman developed his character further than the script did in the 1958 *Playhouse 90* episode entitled "The Last Man": "The story is that Sterling Hayden takes revenge on this town because when he goes to the pharmacy, the pharmacy won't give him pills for his pregnant wife, who is in pain; and she dies. The opening scene, he's in a wagon and trying to get the pharmacist to open up and he won't do it. He takes revenge on this town and recruits a bunch of killers. I was one of them. I was a gunslinger. It was kind of a memorable part for me. John Frankenheimer and I worked very well together. I did a lot of stuff I incorporated into this character — every time I killed somebody, my hands started to sweat. This was my idea. When I take out this bandana, this kerchief I have in my sleeve, and I start wiping my fingers, that was indicative that somebody was going to get bumped off."

Another interesting aspect of this particular episode is that it combined three forms of broadcasting. "That's a combination of live television, film, and tape, within thirty seconds. It was a live show in Hollywood, and they taped horses coming in, and they had a film sequence of about ten or fifteen seconds that had to do with an explosion...It was all incorporated into thirty seconds of a live show. Very effective."

They had special effects even back then, although not to the extent we do now. Richman continues, "There was one particular scene when I killed the store owner and I set a whole bunch of liquid stuff down to blow the place up, then I walk out of the store. I walked the whole length of the studio, the camera's following me, then when I get to Hurd Hatfield (who played Ivers in the show) I get behind him and I tip his hat and strike a match to light my cigarette. When I scratch the match in my fingers, that was the signal to blow the building, way back in the distance. It explodes."

One of actor Steven Marlo's favorites was a 1956 *Studio One* episode entitled "Guiulio." Here's why: "It's a story about an Italian boy who loved opera and he's got a great voice. I played that part. It's kind of a love story. Because I don't have an operatic voice, I had to learn the whole score to 'La Traviata' and mouth it while we had an actor off-stage singing it. He was an operatic singer. We practiced it so that when I opened my mouth, I was in sync with him. I loved that show. It was one of my favorite shows."

The 1957 *Kraft Television Theatre* episode "Most Blessed Woman" stands out in Rance Howard's memory. "It was an excellent script and starred Al Salmi and Betsy von Furstenberg. I played (Furstenberg's) brother. It was a wonderful show, and I had a pretty good role. Another one that stands out in my memory was one called "Sheriff's Man." I played a young man on the run that was in pursuit by the law."

Jack Benny, like many other comedians of those days, had come from radio. Being accustomed to a radio station, the cameras were distracting to him, so they placed them in the back of the room, behind the studio audience, and turned off their red-light signals. Benny was a very unusual, wonderful man. He was the opposite of his tightwad image — overtipping and considerate of those around him. In return, his staff was very loyal to him. He always censored himself, avoiding hurtful, political or dirty lines or themes. He gauged the success of a joke by the audience's reaction, so the live-TV format with an audience was perfect for his needs.

Sid Caesar was another performer who blossomed before an audience. Many of his show's skits have become legendary. "This Is Your Story", a spoof of the popular *This is Your Life* television show, was among their best. In this skit, Howard Morris was given free rein to ad lib to his heart's content, and he seemed to have a grand old time doing so. Watching Tarzan movies gave him all the inspiration he needed. As emcee Carl Reiner tried to keep order, Morris' long-lost Uncle Goofy character tearfully clung to Caesar like Cheetah. With a sparkle in his eye, Morris later said that, had Caesar's back held out, they would still be doing that sketch.

* * *

Unions had become very important to people involved in television broadcasting by this time. What began as the American Federation of Radio Artists (AFRA) merged in 1952 with the Television Authority to form the American Federation of Television and Radio Artists (AFTRA). This was the organization that won the much-needed health and retirement benefits for its members just two years later. Actors can depend on their union to have their best interests at heart.

Others had their unions, as well. Technical employees had the Association of Technical Employees (ATE). Once this group broadened its membership to include technicians in radio, film, and television, its initials became NABET-CWA. Directors, assistant directors, and stage managers had the Directors Guild of America (DGA), writers had the Writers Guild of America (WGA), and musicians had the American Federation of Musicians (AFM).

All of these organizations made life a little (sometimes a lot) easier for its members.

The Andrews Sisters on *The Frank Sinatra Show*

Peggy Ann Garner and Francis L. Sullivan on *Schlitz Playhouse of the Stars*

Eve Arden

Harvey Stephens, Martha Hyer, and David Niven on *Four Star Playhouse*

Nina Foch in *Philco Television Playhouse*

Joan Tetzel and Sir Cedric Hardwicke on *Climax!*

Skip Homeier and Margaret O'Brien on *Lux Video Theatre* FROM THE COLLECTION OF RODOLFO CARREON

Janet Leigh on *Schlitz Playhouse of Stars* FROM THE COLLECTION OF RODOLFO CARREON

Wright King as Sam Clemens in *The Gabby Hayes Show*, directed by Vincent Donohue. 2/21/51

Wright King, featured in *The Gabby Hayes Show* on live TV, 1950. Sam Bass, episode written by Jerome Coopersmith (photgraphed from a kinescope).

PART TWO

CHAPTER FIVE

FOR ALL YOU KIDDIES OUT THERE

Don Herbert (aka "Mr. Wizard") and Bruce Lindgren
performing a science experiment

While we were writing this book, a television legend passed from our midst. Don Herbert, otherwise known as Mr. Wizard, succumbed to bone cancer. He didn't go without leaving us a wonderful legacy, however. He took the aura of mystery out of science and brought it into our homes. With a boy or girl by his side, he conducted experiments, teaching that child and us that science was in our lives every day. He taught us how to think and reason like a scientist. The first few years, beginning in 1951, this Peabody Award-winning show was aired live. Combine the "no retakes" format with the elements of fire, water, and air, and you have the potential for the unexpected. Children were glued to their sets every Saturday at noon. Perhaps Mr. Wizard's calm, reasoning approach touched them more effectively than their classroom teachers, and many of these children went on to make science their careers. Host Bill Nye of the Emmy-winning series *Bill Nye the Science Guy*, says on the *www.skeptic.com* website, "Don Herbert's techniques and performances helped create the

SOUPY SALES

STARRING:
*Soupy Sales
Clyde Adler*

PREMISE:
Children's comedy show with puns, puppets, and slapstick.

HOWDY DOODY

STARRING:
*Bob Smith
Alfie Scopp
Bob Keeshan
Mack Mather (voice)
Claude Rae (voice)*

PREMISE:
Long-running Children's show with puppet characters and kids in the "Peanut Gallery."

United States's first generation of homegrown rocket scientists just in time to respond to Sputnik. He sent us to the Moon. He changed the world."

* * *

Wright, you appeared as Midshipman Bascomb on *Captain Video and His Video Rangers* on the Du Mont network, didn't you? What do you remember about that?

That was a commitment of maybe a week or two of daily performances. The floor manager had an identical twin brother who one day had his earphones and other gear on, mimicking the real guy. He appeared before the control booth and, in a phony show of rage during the actual broadcast, tore his earphones and other important equipment off, practically giving the director a stroke.

So children's shows weren't immune to pranks. Many of us have heard of another such thing on Soupy Sales' show when there was a knock at his door and he opened it. Unseen to the audience, but

While Buffalo Bob and Howdy Doody are entertaining their young audience, we see them from a different angle.

in full view of Sales, was a nude woman. What a relief when he later realized the audience hadn't seen that!

Children's programming in these years often included puppets and marionettes. It was very wholesome programming. *Howdy Doody* began in 1947 and was first given a circus atmosphere, then later settled down in "Doodyville." The main puppet, Howdy, evolved over the years as well, being a smiling cowboy by the time my family got its first television set in 1955. Buffalo Bob Smith was a charismatic host, giving the show a feeling of excitement with his exuberant "Say, kids, what time is it?" The kids in the Peanut Gallery, as well as at home, would then respond with glee, "It's Howdy Doody time!" It's probably pretty much common knowledge now that one of the actors who portrayed the mute clown Clarabell was none other than Bob Keeshan, the future Captain Kangaroo. Keeshan learned much from his experiences on other children's shows, enabling him to put forth a quality program of his own soon after.

Wright, you starred as a regular in a children's show early in your career. Even though this occurred during the live-TV era, I understand it was filmed.

That's correct. *Johnny Jupiter* had originally been aired live when it was broadcast from the Du Mont network in early 1953 and starred Vaughn Taylor. After a while, ABC took over and decided to film the show and have a younger actor — me — take Taylor's place. The Jupiterians were portrayed by puppets. Videotapes are available of the filmed version, but it's very difficult — perhaps impossible — to find kinescopes of the live version now. Vaughn was a good friend. I worked in both New York and Hollywood with him. He was an excellent actor with a dry sense of humor.

Mork and Mindy, a couple decades later, seemed to have adopted some of the *Johnny Jupiter* premise. The 1950s show was a satire whose central character was the human custodian Earnest P. Duckweather, who interacted with the Jupiterians by way of a seemingly magic television set. Trying to adequately explain to the aliens why Earthlings do what they do, especially since all they knew of us was what they saw on network television, was no easy task. Even though this live series got great reviews, it didn't have a sponsor and the Du Mont network wasn't

The live version of *Johnny Jupiter* with Vaughn Taylor

strong enough to sustain it while it established an audience. Consequently, it was cancelled after only three months.

ABC realized what a fine show it was and picked it up, restructuring it as children's show.

Another good children's show in those days was *Ding Dong School*. Dr. Frances Horwich seems to have served her viewers very much like Mr. Wizard did. She, too, was a gifted teacher who cared deeply for children. She was perhaps the first to speak directly to the viewers. So excellent was this show that some kindergartens brought a TV set into their classrooms so the children could watch Miss Frances.

Young viewers loved Miss Frances

The Pinky Lee Show lasted only two years because of the star's ill health, but made an indelible impression on 1950s kids. Quite outlandish when compared to other children's programs of the day, it became the apparent model for *Pee Wee's Playhouse* thirty years later.

Sadly, none of the stars of these live-broadcasted children's shows is still with us. How fun it would have been to hear their memories of those long-ago days!

Writer S. L. Kotar, who lived in upstate New York at the time, participated in a children's show on Schenectady's WRGB a few times. Many people thought of it as *The Freddie Freihofer Show* because the sponsor, Freihofer's Baking Company, was advertised throughout the show; but its proper title was *Breadtime Story*. Airing from 5:15 to 5:30, it was WRGB's first local children's show, and featured a very gifted artist. "A kid would make a scribble on his pad and he ("Uncle" Jim Fisk) would use that as the start of a picture — like a dog or a cat," Kotar recalls. There were several men who served in this capacity. In addition to Fisk, there was Ralph Kanna, Ed Joyce, and Harry "Bud" Mason. It was Kanna who would make art his career, later creating a comic strip for *The Hartford Times*, in collaboration with fellow artist Jim Aparo, and starting the RK Art School for aspiring cartoonists. "I remember we sat on short bleachers and there were probably 25 kids per show. The sponsor was Freihofer's, the local bakery (still going strong) and they gave you free cookies after the show. My big remembrance was that the lights were hot!" *Breadtime Story* was a very successful show, airing from 1949 to 1966.

* * *

One of the most memorable farewells in television history came on the very last episode of *Howdy Doody*. This is when Clarabell spoke for the only time, saying "Good-bye, kids."

Clarabell the Clown

CHAPTER SIX

STAY TUNED FOR NEWS

In 1947, the newsman whose face would someday be as familiar to Los Angeles viewers as their own reported for his first day of work at KTLA. What Stan Chambers discovered was a garage that had been converted into a television broadcasting studio. The lights were hung from wooden rafters and they had just one stage, which was individualized with furniture and props to suit each show. To the front of the stage were several rows of folding chairs for their audience. The two cameras were very big and clunky. There were no specialist positions; everyone had a variety of duties to perform. Just as Paul Harvey does today, the news anchor would also do the commercials.

Until then, viewers had been accustomed to getting their news from radio or the weekly newsreels at movie theaters. KTLA would, in fact, often get its news footage from newsreels during those early days. By the time Hearst Metrotone News video clips were copied and sent to the west coast, the picture was still good but the sound was very bad, so they would just run the visuals and narrate it themselves.

The teleprompter helped the news reader to maintain eye contact with the camera. The top of the teleprompter was right below the lens, so it appeared to the viewer that the newsman was looking directly at him. A stagehand would roll the text manually.

The only air conditioning was in the control room. It had to be relatively cool there because the electronic equipment needed to be kept from overheating.

If a reporter wanted to interview on camera people who were at the scene when news happened, they had to come to the studio to do it. Equipment was not portable then. That was soon to change.

The remote broadcast was invented by Klaus Landsberg, also of KTLA, when a huge explosion rocked downtown Los Angeles. As it turned out, that was a prelude to an even bigger story to come. In April, 1949, a tiny three-year-old girl named Kathy Fiscus had fallen far, far down an unused water well and was trapped. KTLA was on the spot to report the rescue attempt in San Marino. News of little Kathy's dilemma spread around the world. Time stood still as everyone who heard about it prayed for Kathy and were glued to the nearest television set to watch the progress of the rescuers.

Movie studios had loaned their powerful klieg lights to the effort, making the nighttime scene as bright as day. For twenty-seven hours Chambers and his partner Bill Welsh shared reporting duties. As one was on camera, the other was walking around, gathering more information. All the manpower and concern expended was for naught, however. When they finally reached little Kathy, she was dead.

This was the first extended-period coverage of an event that pre-empted regular programming, and would be repeated many times in the future when events of monumental importance occurred. Big news and its live coverage would supersede everything else, even commercials. Money didn't set the rules back then.

In those days, the news media was considerate and allowed those making the news to maintain their dignity. Reporters were respectful of families' privacy.

Each week, KTLA had a show called "City at Night," which would show its audience the behind-the-scenes goings on inside various businesses around town. Once, they were visiting Fire Station 27 in Hollywood. At first, all was fine on this tour. Then the alarm sounded and the fire fighters piled into the fire engines and rushed to the scene, leaving the reporter with only one fire chief to interview. The interesting visuals were gone.

News innovator Klaus Landsburg COURTESY OF LARRY BLOOMFIELD, KA6UTC

The 1951 return of soldiers from the Korean War occurred about one hundred miles from Los Angeles. Remote coverage from that far away had never been done before, but Klaus Landsburg's can-do attitude made it happen.

When atomic bomb tests were scheduled in Nevada in 1952, the networks decided not to televise it. They felt it would be too cumbersome and expensive, and there wasn't enough time to prepare. Landsberg felt differently. He worked hard to pull it off and, with the help of the Marines and their heavy-duty helicopters, he did it. On April 22, 1952, KTLA accomplished what the networks couldn't. Their heavy equipment was atop the mountain, along with their reporters, in spite of a sandstorm and blizzard.

While preparing to cover a Fourth of July fireworks celebration in 1953 from an aircraft carrier, Landsberg wondered if the festivities could be shown from the vantage point of the Navy helicopter. They tried it. The camera was connected to its base of operations with a one-hundred-fifty-foot cable, so the copter went up fifty feet, leaving one hundred feet of cable to spare. It was quite a fine view from up there!

Later, they would develop the ability to have miniature equipment on board without the dangling cable, so the copter would become a self-contained broadcasting studio. Again KTLA was the trailblazer. Their Bell telecopter of 1958 would make birds-eye reporting commonplace in the following decades.

Stan Chambers, who has been in the business for decades and is still employed by KTLA, wrote a wonderful book about his experiences. It is entitled *News at Ten: Fifty Years with Stan Chambers*. In one chapter, he sets forth his theory of why there is so much nostalgia for the 1950s these days. Life was much simpler back then, and there was an air of optimism enjoyed by the generation that had won a world war and was now back home and living the good life. So different from the 2000s, when unpredictability and instability are the norm. Much of the news of the 1950s would be considered boring by today's standards.

Oh, for those "boring" days again!

STAY TUNED FOR NEWS

CHAPTER SEVEN

IT'S GAME TIME!

After seeing him in *The Twilight Zone, Gunsmoke, Wanted Dead or Alive,* and other such shows, as well as dramatic and sci-fi movies, you might think of Wright King as a very serious dramatic actor. If you didn't see him on the Broadway stage, you're sure to have watched him on television many times over the years. But did you know he appeared also on a game show? Tell us about that, Wright.

A game show of this long-ago era was entitled *Say It With Acting*, a program hosted by the then famous NBC personality Ben Grauer. He was a wonderful host to a beautiful introduction into live TV. Aired on Sunday evenings, it pitted two teams against each other. Each team consisted of four cast members of a current Broadway play, and they competed with the other team to guess the answers to questions about the theatre through a game of charades. We won. A record of four times!!! The one incident I remember most, appearing on it for the second of the four times straight with my cast mates, was October 30, 1949. Our first child, Wright Jr., was born on that day. The entire studio audience and casts were highly enthusiastic at my good news.

One of my all-time favorite game shows was *Masquerade Party*, in which celebrities came out in costumes that would both disguise them and also be a clue to their identities. Most memorable was when my childhood idol, Lloyd Bridges, came out in complete SCUBA gear. Since his hit show at the time was *Sea Hunt*, I'm guessing it took all of five seconds for the panel to guess that one. This show ended up airing on each of the three major networks at one time or another during its eight-year run.

All the game shows in which lovely young actress Betsy Palmer served as panelist were aired live, and she found that *I've Got a Secret*'s success was largely due to the personalities on the panel and their interaction. With Henry Morgan, Bill Cullen, and Bess Myerson joining her on the panel and Gary Moore as host, the chemistry was perfect. "Henry Morgan was the acid and I was the sugar," says Betsy.

I've Got a Secret was one of the era's most-loved game shows. A guest would be presented to the panel, he would whisper his secret into Gary Moore's ear while it appeared simultaneously on the viewers' TV screens, then the panel would be allowed to ask questions that would help them in guessing the secret. One of the most historically significant guests on this show was an elderly gentleman whose secret was that he was there at the Ford Theater when President Lincoln was shot. Turns out the lad was only five years old at the time and hadn't understood what all the commotion was about.

Panelist Henry Morgan assured an interviewer that the secrets were real. Well, sort of. When they didn't have any really good secrets that week, they'd manufacture one. An example: beautiful Ann Sheridan's secret was that she was going to the Belgian Congo and taking Henry Morgan with her. He was completely unaware of those plans, but the producers made sure they were carried out.

Garry Moore and the panel of *I've Got a Secret*

What's My Line had a game plan similar to that of *I've Got a Secret*, except, of course, it was the guest's profession that the panel needed to guess. Another similarity was the chemistry on the panel. Dorothy Kilgallen was a newspaper columnist with plenty of drive and ambition. (It was, in fact, her relentless quest to expose the Kennedy assassination years later as a conspiracy that led many people to feel that her death was murder, rather than suicide.) To achieve a balance that would be pleasing to the audience, Arlene Francis was also a regular panelist. Francis was warm and gracious — the "sugar" to Kilgallen's "acid."

Veteran radio comic Fred Allen worked for a time on the game show *What's My Line?*, and was very surprised to discover that fellow puzzle solvers Francis and Kilgallen actually played to win! About the fourth member of the panel, Bennett Cerf, he said, in true Fred Allen style, "Oh, he's just a tweed wastebasket."

One of the most entertaining question-and-answer sessions on *What's My Line* occurred when the mystery guest was artist Salvador Dali. The panel that evening was blindfolded. A multitalented man, Dali answered in the affirmative when asked if he was a performer in the arts, a leading man, a cartoonist, involved in sports/athletics, and author of a book published by Cerf's firm Random House. This greatly frustrated host John Daly, who wanted the answers to be accurate, but not misleading. Instead of becoming upset, however, his playful nature took hold. In the final minute of the game, Arlene Francis and Dorothy Kilgallen finally figured it out, asking if their guest could be easily recognized by his mustache.

Bud Collyer was the host of the hit game show *Beat the Clock*, which had begun on radio before transitioning into television. The contestants were selected from the audience, and their goal was to perform a stunt of some sort within a certain amount of time, as the seconds ticked off. It was often a simple task with a twist — batting a ball while blindfolded, for instance. The writers would come up with the stunts, and they'd hire unemployed actors to test them out before trying them on the air. They wanted to be sure it was neither too difficult, nor too easy. One of these unemployed actors was James Dean, who could easily perform just about anything they threw at him.

John Daly and the panel of *What's My Line?*

When *The Price is Right* originally aired, it had little of the manic aspect that you see today. The host was Bill Cullen, and the well-dressed contestants sat calmly at a long table, just as panels did on other game shows. An item would be shown to them, and they would place "bids." Whoever came closest to the retail price of the item without going over won the item. No flashing lights, no hysterics, no dislocated limbs. Just a calm, dignified game that we could play along with as we watched.

Then there was *The $64,000 Question*, in which one contestant at a time would be presented to the audience and asked questions in his/her area of expertise by host Hal March. The questions would become progressively more difficult as the dollar amount of the prize doubled each time. The contestant viewers probably remember most is Joyce Brothers. Dr. Brothers' topic of choice was, of all things, boxing! Intelligent lady that she is, she knew an odd combination of contestant-and-topic would increase her chances of being chosen to appear on the program, so she studied up diligently on the topic and achieved the desired results and the ultimate prize of $64,000. It was in the third year of this show that the quiz-show scandal put an end to them all.

It centered on the show *Twenty One*. Two contestants would be placed in isolation booths, in which they could see neither the opponent nor the audience, and could hear only the host Jack Barry when he was speaking directly to them. The difficulty of the questions was relative to their score-points, and the players were unaware of the total points earned by their opponent. The goal was to come closer to 21 points than the other player. One particular player soon grabbed the audience's attention and held them mesmerized. His name was Charles Van Doren, the young, handsome, intellectual son of poet Mark Van Doren and novelist Dorothy Van Doren. Until he came on the scene, Herb Stempel had been winning the game week after week, but the number of viewers was diminishing. In order to keep this charismatic newcomer on the show, the producers instructed that he be given the answers to the questions, and the show's ratings began to climb. Stempel and others saw what had happened and made the situation public. Van Doren admitted wrongdoing before the House Subcommittee on Legislative Oversight, of the United States Senate. Here is his testimony:

> I was involved, deeply involved, in a deception. The fact that I, too, was very much deceived cannot keep me from being the principal victim of that deception, because I was its principal symbol. There may be a kind of justice in that. I don't know. I do know, and I can say it proudly to this committee, that since Friday, October 16, when I finally came to a full understanding of what I had done and of what I must do, I have taken a number of steps toward trying to make up for it.

> I have a long way to go. I have deceived my friends, and I had millions of them. Whatever their feeling for me now, my affection for them is stronger today than ever before. I am making this statement because of them. I hope my being here will serve them well and lastingly.

> ...I asked (co-producer Albert Freedman) to let me go on (*Twenty-One*) honestly, without receiving help. He said that was impossible. He told me that I would not have a chance to defeat Stempel because he was too knowledgeable. He also told me that the show was merely entertainment and that giving help to quiz contests was a common practice and merely a part of show business. This of course was not true, but perhaps I wanted to believe him. He also stressed the fact that by appearing on a nationally televised program I would be doing a great service to the intellectual life, to teachers and to education in general, by increasing public respect for the work of the mind through my performances.

In fact, I think I have done a disservice to all of them. I deeply regret this, since I believe nothing is of more vital importance to our civilization than education.

Several shows of the day, in fact, were guilty of this practice, and it hadn't been considered illegal at the time. Once the cheating was revealed, however, the shows, hosts, and contestants lost their credibility. It would be decades before we would see quiz shows on prime time again.

CHAPTER EIGHT

AND NOW A WORD FROM OUR SPONSOR

Anthology dramas were written in three acts, just as most stage plays are, and commercials were presented during the intermissions. Most shows would have only one sponsor back then.

Commercials were often done live right there in the same studio. Sometimes they were incorporated into the story line of the show and delivered by the show's star. Other times, they weren't. At such times, the person doing the commercial would often be off to the side before a drop curtain, away from the action. For a half-hour show, there would be about two commercials. For an hour-long show, three or four.

The Philip Morris company got a real bargain when they were sponsoring *I Love Lucy*. Not only would their commercials be aired at appropriate times, but also Lucy and Ricky Ricardo would light up their Philip Morris Morris cigarettes now and then during the show.

Unless the sponsoring cigarette was Lucky Strike, the dialog of a show was not allowed to have the word "lucky" in it. The competing cigarette manufacturers didn't want their sponsored shows to be inadvertently pushing the wrong brand.

What were your experiences with commercials of that era, Wright?

I won't forget my first encounter with a live TV commercial. After rehearsing for over a week on my first *Studio One*, I'd found myself with other cast members on CBS's sound stage. While walking, discovering our different sets for our "Lonely Boy" production, I wondered why our play had a kitchen. I guessed it was the one scene I wasn't in. Then I came upon a very familiar face — Betty Furness! I had seen her many times in the movies and now here she was in person right before me in our kitchen. Wrong! The kitchen turned out to be hers — her Westinghouse commercial set. I hadn't owned a television set at the time, so I knew nothing about her Westinghouse commercials. Betty, a total person and actress. Visits with her were a happy part of the times I was on *Studio One*.

When it comes to live commercials, Betty Furness was among America's

best-known saleswoman. What some people might not realize is that she began as an actress.

She, in fact, had appeared in that capacity on *Studio One*. Then she saw that the ladies they originally hired to do their commercials were radio actresses who weren't accustomed to cameras and memory work. She could do it better than that, she thought. And, by golly, she did — for the next eleven-plus years. Westinghouse was their sponsor, and Furness became synonymous with that product, demonstrating with ease their latest model of refrigerator, oven, or whatever. This worked out perfectly for her since she didn't consider herself a great actress. Now she was able to relate to the viewers as a friend. There was no firm contract at first, no exclusivity. She never did a commercial for any other product, however.

Betty Furness would get her script on Friday. The rehearsal with the cameras was on Monday, the dress rehearsal was in the afternoon, and airtime was 10:00. Emotions were high and everyone was excited. She feels the show presented good plays that were beautifully performed. "Everything they did had real integrity," she said. "It was good drama, it was well produced, it had… good directors and beautiful scripts."

According to director Lela Swift, obtaining Westinghouse's sponsorship made the biggest difference in the show. The material became less risky, but the quality was still excellent.

There would be one three-minute and two one-and-a-half minute commercials on each show, and no commercial was ever repeated. Furness' favorite was the refrigerator commercial with tongue-twisting words. The one about a jet engine was a true challenge for her. She knew it wouldn't be believable for her to know all about such things, so she reworded it to say, "They tell me this is how it works…"

For the commercials, they used two to three cameras, just as they did for the drama. The commercials had a different director than the drama did, and he wanted Furness to wear a wedding ring because she was talking to viewers who were housewives. She refused. "Ad agencies tend to be very scared," she said. "I wasn't scared." She wore her own clothes, taking care not to wear the same outfit again too soon. When she wore a chemise or other fashionable dress, the sponsor thought it was too distracting and wanted her to dress like a plain housewife. She again refused and prevailed. She was right, too. It showed the product in a better light if a stylishly-dressed woman was demonstrating it, rather than a dowdy housewife. It's not logical, but is it true that a well-dressed person usually appears more intelligent than a sloppily-dressed one.

The commercials were separated from the drama by music, so Furness didn't try to let the storyline influence the commercial. Sometimes she would, though, especially during political conventions. There was more leeway there, fewer time constraints. Many people had bought television sets in 1952 for the primary purpose of watching the political conventions. Westinghouse was the sole sponsor of this event, so she got more airtime than any of the politicians. Early in her career, Furness had hoped to someday be a political delegate. This, to her, was the next-best thing.

There was a blooper in 1954 that was attributed to Betty Furness, but she says it was really someone else. June Graham, her stand-by, did the commercial in which the refrigerator wouldn't open because it wasn't plugged in. They then did a close-up of the refrigerator while a stagehand plugged it in. The door then opened, and the camera pulled back.

Another blooper was indeed experienced by Furness. She was to demonstrate a tank vacuum cleaner, showing how easy it was to take the toss-away bag out and replace it, but she couldn't get the lid off. It had been put on so tightly that even the men couldn't get it off later. Consequently, she just told about it instead of showing it.

Furness' Paley Center interviewer, Loring Mandel, recalled that the brash Henry Morgan was doing an Admiral refrigerator commercial once but couldn't get the door open. In frustration, he said "Get a Frigidaire" and walked off. He was fired from the program.

One particularly uncomfortable situation occurred during the episode that featured the drama "Judgment at Nuremberg." Furness' commercial about a gas oven came right after the dramatic scene of a gas chamber in a prison camp with a corpse inside!

* * *

Director Kenneth Whelan had many hilarious things to say about his experiences in live television in his book, *How The Golden Age of Television Turned My Hair to Silver*. Some of the shows he was involved in were real losers; but one daytime show, *The Garry Moore Show*, a comedy-variety show premiering in 1950, rated extremely high on his scale. The people involved — all of them — were very professional and kind. Like the later *The Andy Griffith Show*, the star of the show was the "reactor" while it was the sidekick who was the comic relief. Durwood Kirby served as Moore's sidekick. Garry was a warm, affectionate man, and that's the winning qualities he gave to his show. He and the cast gave it a family feel.

Moore encouraged live commercials, frequently doing them as humorous sketches with Kirby. He refused, however, to advertise a product he didn't believe in. Whelan describes a carpet commercial that he knew from the beginning would be a fiasco. The idea was for a baby to be sitting on the carpet, playing with his toys, when a dog comes in, licks the baby's face, and sits beside him. A baby and dog performing in a predictable way on live television? Not likely! Just put some bacon grease on the baby's face to attract the dog and it'll work out just fine, they assured him. Whelan had visions of the dog eating the baby's well-greased head. Nevertheless, it would soon be air time, so they had to go ahead with it. The camera focused on the lovely carpet, then panned over to the baby, who was not playing with any toys. He was just staring up at the camera, as grease dripped from his chin, "making the baby look like a well-basted turkey ready to be popped into the oven," wrote Whelan. After staring at the camera for a while, the baby then toppled over onto his side and began crying. The dog came in, but, instead of going over to the baby, he zipped across the soundstage to camera three, "which he used for a hydrant." The dog was on the air for about a second. The remaining forty seconds were devoted to focusing back on the lovely carpet.

Now we understand why actors don't like to work with children or animals.

* * *

The setting of a live television show was fertile ground for bloopers, so let's devote a whole chapter to that topic.

CHAPTER NINE

BLOOPERS

Live television was a goldmine of bloopers. How could it not be, with no second chances given?

The ultimate situation that went awry was a tragic one in which British actor Gareth Jones died of a massive heart attack during the *Armchair Theatre* presentation of "Underground," mercifully off-camera. Obviously, much improvisation had to be done to get through the rest of the show. During the commercial break, his co-stars were told that he had fallen and gotten hurt. It was only after the show was over that they were told the truth.

Most people seem to love bloopers, though. Maybe it's because it demonstrates that actors aren't that much different from their viewers. Things go wrong. They make mistakes. Those unplanned "emergencies" can be entertaining, though, and — Hey, actors *are* entertainers, after all. So what are some lighthearted bloopers you remember from your live TV days, Wright?

One of the most surreal presentations of the new 1951 series *Out There* was its premiere episode. The curious audience was awaiting an introduction into a new world. They were given just that by our cast — via the first act, THIRD (!) act, and second act of the production, in that order! VVVEEERRRYYY surreal.

Then, in the *Studio One* drama called "The Dangerous Years," there was a dialog between Wright and Harry Townes when we viewers heard an off-camera noise, like a dish that was dropped. A stagehand might have been getting the commercial ready and dropped a prop. Realizing the story was more important than the noise, the actors ignored the clamor and kept right on as if it hadn't happened. Stage training certainly did come in handy in live TV.

On live TV there were no "cuts" or spared angles where the gunman could fire a pistol in what could appear as a direct shot. On a *Matinee Theatre* western I, portraying the heavy, had to aim and shoot directly to the nearby bargirl, gorgeous Cloris Leachman. In rehearsal a "Click!" was the only response from my pistol. On the air it had to fire an actual shot. The prop man assured our director that a full load (cap) was too much for such a close firing, and so instead of a full report, my pistol would fire a quarter load. When I shot the pistol during the actual event, Miss Leachman

received instead the stunning impact of a *half* load. Not a tragedy, but certainly a shock and minor powder burns to our leading lady.

This next anecdote isn't a blooper really, but illustrates that things sometimes go wrong before the show is aired. In August of 1952, we had been rehearsing a Lillian Hellman play for *Broadway Television Theatre* for several days when it was discovered that we didn't have the rights to it. Consequently, the producer, Warren Wade, was forced to locate a substitute script. We were to do a completely different script in only three days' time! <u>Only</u> three days rehearsal time to learn and perform a three-act farce, the "Three Cornered Moon." Surprisingly, the first night came off beautifully. *Broadway Television Theatre* was live television, but at station WOR we performed the play as in summer stock — five performances a week. The second night, nothing!! We simply learned the lines so quickly that they hadn't stuck to our memories. Back to the rehearsals...we studied with care...and all was fine...but it was a jarring lesson.

Warren Wade had been an important department head in radio at NBC before moving over to television. After working in the area of casting for NBC for a while, he came to WOR-TV, where he worked on *Broadway Television Theatre*. He was a man who got things done, sometimes with the veiled threat to the director and crew, "Well, fellas, I guess we'll just have to go to film," to which most would protest, "Oh, no, Mr. Wade! We'll find a way!" Everyone then worked harder to get the show in letter-perfect shape. This series would present the same show every night for five nights. This was the kind of system that was ideal. One thing I admired about Wade was that, by sometimes using certain actors in his plays, he revived some whose careers had been sagging.

Danger, a popular weekly half-hour drama directed by famed director Sidney Lumet, presented a terse story involving two mountaineers portrayed by a character actor and myself as his son in a conflict with a lost hunter, played by Richard Kiley. All went well in the early moments, until Kiley's entrance, at which time the character actor/father drew a blank, forgetting most of his lines, leaving Kiley and myself to frantically improvise the remainder of the play before my silent mountaineer father. Faulty memories — forgetting lines, an actor's worst nightmare. Maybe that should be the title of this chapter.

Sometimes, when an actor forgot a line and his cast mates weren't able to cue him, the audio portion of the show would be momentarily turned off while the stage manager would give the actor his line. To the viewing audience, it just seemed as if the station was having mechanical difficulties for a few seconds.

You've heard the phrase "dead man walking," haven't you? That happened many times in live TV. The actor, after being "killed," thinking the camera was now focused in another direction, rose and walked off the set — only to discover later that the viewers at home witnessed that amazing resurrection.

We all have our bloopers-stories to tell, so let's call on other folks in the business and see what whoppers they most remember.

Bill Erwin (actor best known for the beloved film *Somewhere in Time* and his *Twilight Zone* appearances): "My favorite story from the old days — I forget which show was being done live in New York but some great woman star and a young man are seated in an airliner. The young man 'went up on his lines,'* so he stood up, said 'This is where I get off.' Then he walked to the door and exited. I'm sure the control room went crazy, but somehow they continued the scene. I'm sure they never called the young actor again.

Says **Jack Klugman**, the female star of that drama was Eva Marie Saint. The actor, after making his exit, went to the back, got his line, then returned, saying "I was only kidding."

Each person seems to remember this flub a bit differently. Here's how **Eva Marie Saint** tells it: "The TV Show was a series called *One Man's Family*. Yes, the actor forgot his lines and drew a blank. He looked straight into the camera and announced, '…I've blown the scene.' We were in a plane and I just leaned against the window and said, 'Father Roberts, I think I'll take a nap.' Of course, the director quickly went to the commercial. During that time, I reminded the actor of his lines, and after the commercial we resumed the scene. Yes, it was a scary situation…It was one of *many* on *live TV!* It was an exciting time."

Betsy Palmer: "There was one show I was doing, it might've been a *Studio One*, and the cyc [cyclorama] — because in these little studios, they were just little old movie houses and theaters, and the walls were all brick, so they had to hang this material to cover them in case the camera shot off the set, so you wouldn't look at a brick wall. You'd just see blank, and that would be the cyc. I remember we were doing the show and the cyc caught fire. They had rows of lights underneath to keep them lit up to a color of sorts, and that had set fire to it. There we were in the middle of a show, the darn thing was burning and smoking. They brought in water from outside somewhere and the hose. I was running in water up to my ankles to change. The woman was taking my blouse off. In those days, we girls always wore underwear because you had to change your clothes right there on the floor, while all of it was going on. I remember thinking, 'I'm going to die. I'm going to die. We're all going to die'."

Jack Klugman: This fun blooper happened on *Philco Television Playhouse*, an anthology series produced by Fred Coe. Klugman says, "I remember in one show I was in jail, and the guy in the cell opposite me threw a gun my

---

*"Going up" on one's lines means the actor has forgotten his dialog.

way and I was supposed to pick it up, and then they would go to black — but it didn't reach me! I couldn't get it. All of a sudden a foot came in and just kicked the gun [in my direction]."

Don Grady: "I was singing one of my songs at the piano on *The Tonight Show*...I was nervous, my mouth was kind of dry, and as soon as I opened it to sing, my upper lip got hung up on my front teeth...you know, from being so dry. I couldn't get it down, both of my hands were occupied at the piano...so I did most of the song with my top lip curled up on my front teeth! A pretty sight, I'm sure."

Jan Merlin (star of *The Rough Riders*): "I had a couple of my own mishaps, one on each Coast. In New York, when doing the series of *Tom Corbett, Space Cadet*, we were aboard the Polaris in outer space when our Captain was floating helplessly into the far reaches, and we three cadets argued about his rescue. Corbett, the hero, and Astro, the Venusian cadet, wanted to suit up and get him, while I, as Roger Manning, the troublemaker, had a long involved speech to make as to why we should go back to the Academy to get help. During the excitement, Astro demanded, "Do you mean you want to leave Captain Strong out there to die?" I forgot every word of my dialogue and retorted, 'WHY NOT?' It must have rocked all those little kids at home back on their haunches.

Jan Merlin

"On the West Coast, I was playing Oliver Wendell Holmes leading my troops into a Civil War battle in a *Hallmark Hall of Fame* episode 'The Touch of Steel.' All through rehearsals, the large horse pistol I used was kept unloaded and I would say 'Bang' to indicate when I fired the gun. On air, bravely charging toward the camera, I pulled the trigger, and nothing happened, so I shouted 'BANG!' automatically.

"There's not much an actor can do when the show is 'live.' Poor old Boris Karloff was playing a death scene in *Don Quixote*, and as he lay dying in Sancho Panza's lap, the camera dollied in for a full close-up of his dying words...and his mustache sliding down his sweating cheek.

"Which brings to mind that when Lon Chaney Jr. did the Frankenstein monster, he wasn't aware that rehearsals broke for dinner and then the cast came back to do the performance 'live'…and the nation saw the monster stalk down the castle corridor, servants darting away into side rooms, and Lon paused to say, 'Shut the d*** door' as he passed a room entry, and then he lifted a huge chair over his head and looked solemnly into camera to advise his director, 'I'll break it on air.'

"Yep, them was the good ole days…"

Arthur Penn: An unfortunate incident gave Penn one of his big breaks. The production's director had collapsed on the console due to a hemorrhaging ulcer as a show was on the air, so Penn had to take over. It was good policy back then to have spare cameras — and spare directors — around, just in case. It wasn't unusual for a camera to go out, either. On one of the *Philco* shows, two of their three cameras were inoperable at once!

Stan Chambers: Chambers' employer, KTLA, had been the first to discover Lawrence Welk's talent for pleasing an audience and gave him his own show, with Chambers doing the live commercials.

There were four commercials for each show, and he did them with ease. Then the show went national on ABC, and Chambers was to participate in only one commercial, still aired live. Dodge was the sponsor, and his part in this particular commercial was to walk down the stairs while looking admiringly at the car, get into it, then drive smoothly off while Lon Crosby narrated off-camera. Simple enough. Chambers' cue came, and he walked down the stairs, then slipped suavely into the car. He turned the ignition and tried to drive off, but the car made a jerky start, bucking and stopping several times before finally allowing itself to be driven off. Chambers feels that there was nothing wrong with the car, but its balkiness was due to his own uncharacteristic nervousness.

Lawrence Welk

Rance Howard: "I didn't witness this, but I'm sure this happened. It was a classic. They were doing a program about an Air Force story. There was an actor sitting in the cockpit of the plane and suddenly went blank. Totally forgetting his dialog, he just sat there. The director realized what had happened. It was about time for the commercial anyway, so he cut away to the commercial. Now the commercials were also done live. It caught the [announcer] who was standing by to do the commercial off-guard. Suddenly, he looked up and the [camera's] red light was on him, and he started trying to do the commercial and fumbling around. The director realized that <u>that</u> actor was in serious trouble also! So he thought maybe the actor who was sitting in the cockpit had remembered his line and could resume the scene, so he switched the camera back to the cockpit. The actor sitting in the cockpit was shaking his head and saying 'Twenty years in the legitimate theatre and I've never flubbed a line. I never flubbed a line!' He then looked up and saw the red light was on him!"

Albert Salmi: From his memoirs: "I'd like to relate a tale of live TV in which I starred with a man who was also highly regarded as an actor. [Michael Rennie was the other actor, and they were appearing in the *Climax!* episode entitled "The Volcano Seat"] Basically, the plot was of the in-flight fueling of other aircraft. We were the fuel plane and, during one fueling, the fuel bulkhead was punctured and we had to bring the plane in very slowly and totally level. If the plane wasn't level, if the nose was up, the liquid fuel would run to the tail and we would stall and go down tail first. If the nose of the plane was down, the fuel would slosh forward and we would dive to our deaths. It was a simple story, and, coupled with stock shots of the plane in flight, we could carry out the story believably.

"We rehearsed three weeks first the fueling of fighter planes. They got into a row and one by one came in, hooked up, got the fuel hooked, and the next plane took its place. Then the accident! Then the tense, careful flying to land, staying level all the way. Finally, braking very slowly on landing to prevent the gasoline from slamming forward. We would have little scenes and then go to the stock shot showing the plane in flight, then in the studio another scene, gingerly leveling the plane, watching the speed, then the stock shot of the plane, then the scene in the studio of turning slowly and level to return to the field, then the stock shot of the plane turning, then back to the studio explaining to the control tower our problem, back to stock shot, then in the cockpit where the two men speak of their lives and their dreams, then the stock shot of the plane. This goes on and on for an hour, and we finally land safely and the tower says, 'Well done.'

"The technical rehearsal went very well. It was stop-and-go to make sure all the ducks were in a row, lighting good, shadows good, projection of the sky and clouds good, handling of instruments good, everything fine. We broke for dinner, then back to the studio and into the realistic mock-up of the plane's cockpit for the dress rehearsal. This began with the normal 'ten seconds, nine, eight, seven, six, five, four, three, two.' And then the floor manager points and we begin the play. This we did. We played the first little scene, then we knew they went to the stock shot of the plane, then the signal from the floor manager, we played the next scene, and so on.

"About five minutes into the play, I saw the director come rushing from the control room in a highly agitated way, waving his arms like a demented dervish. My fellow actor and I were astounded and we slid back the cockpit window. We, at first, could not hear what he was saying because of the engine noise, which, of course, was recorded and had not been cut off. Finally, someone cut the engine recording and there stood the director looking up at this mock-up of the plane's cockpit with tears in his eyes, and the words we finally heard were, 'Aren't you going to act for me?' The other actor and I exchanged incredulous stares. We were convinced that the director had lost his mind.

"We finally got the story from him. When they cut to us in the cockpit, we were just sitting there, doing nothing. Then went to stock, they came back to us and there we were, sitting there doing and saying nothing. What had happened was in the initial opening of the dress rehearsal, we misunderstood the floor manager's finger pointing. As it happens, we were playing the scene when they were showing the stock shots and sitting quietly when they were on us. In live TV, the camera that was operating exhibited a red light so the actor knew which camera was live. However, because of the large amount of glass in the plane's windshields, the red lights were disconnected, so we were relying totally on the floor manager. We really could not look at him directly, so we got our cue from large, sweeping arm movements and these we read incorrectly. There was very little time left before the show was to air, so all we did was talk to the floor manager to make sure that we were perfectly clear as to his cues. We assured the director that there would be no more problems. We did the show, everything went swimmingly, scenes played, stock shots, we came to the end, breathed a sigh of relief, got out of our costumes, and went home. Such was the life of a live TV actor."

Incidentally, when this episode was presented a second time on June 12, 1958, the portion in which the men were talking about their lives and dreams was interesting. Salmi's character mentioned being married for two years and having a fourteen-month-old daughter. That was exactly his personal situation at that time — he had been married for two years to actress Peggy Ann Garner and their daughter Catherine was fourteen months old. Ad-libbing was not all that uncommon in live television.

Kathy Garver: "[Our work on *Climax* and *Matinee Theatre*] was like doing a play. You just went on with it. We never stopped. I can see in my head right now a scene we were doing. It was a hot day in Chicago and the fire hydrants spewed out its water [on the soundstage]. That was supposed to happen, but it wasn't supposed to go on quite as long as it did. We were just drenched, but they were standing by with towels when it was over."

Leslie Nielsen (star of the *Naked Gun* movie series and *Airplane!*): Says musical director Irvin Robbin regarding a 1952 episode of *Tales of Tomorrow*, "One catastrophe you can see today on the available video tapes. It was 'Appointment on Mars,' starring a very young Leslie Nielsen. At the end of a tense drama, Nielsen's character has been [shot] by the bad guy as they stand on the Martian surface. The final scene was supposed to show Nielson shooting the bad guy, and then a fade to black from the stony landscape of Mars. The wounded Nielson was supposed to pick up a pistol in the foreground,

Leslie Nielsen

and shoot the other guy upstage, in the background. But the gun wouldn't fire or was empty or was the wrong gun! He pulled the trigger a few times, and then, supposedly dying from his [gunshot] wound, decided to limp and crawl all the way upstage over the rocks to choke the villain to death! It took far longer than in rehearsal, of course, and I sweated out the playing of the final music, which was timed to cover the original scene. Fortunately, it was just long enough, and I was able to hit the act curtain on the fade out." What makes this particular blooper even funnier is the fact that the bad guy was played by burly Brian Keith. That must've been some powerful choke hold for the dying hero to have subdued such a large opponent!

When all else fails, strangle the guy!

Art Carney (Jackie Gleason's sidekick) was a pro. In a "Honeymooners" sketch Jackie had exited through the bedroom door and, a while later, co-star Audrey Meadows went after him. They were supposed to immediately come back together, but they didn't. Gleason, thinking he had more time than he did, had gone to wipe his perspiring forehead. So there it was — no Jackie or Audrey, just Art Carney by himself on stage on live television. Carney then went to the refrigerator and looked for something to eat. While the director and stage manager were in panic, Carney calmly reached into the icebox and retrieved an orange. He sat down at the table and proceeded to peel the orange — no words said, just pantomime. The very relieved director, Kenneth Whelan, felt it was hilarious, and he was simply amazed at the unperturbed Carney's complete trust this his own abilities.

Charlton Heston (Oscar-winning leading man): On *The Philco Television Playhouse* episode "Hear My Heart Speak," Heston played a shell-shocked veteran who was mute. His method of communication was via pencil and paper. The prop man neglected to put paper and pencil in one scene, however, so Heston pantomimed his lines.

Raymond Massey (best known for his convincing portrayal of Abraham Lincoln in various productions): Wright recalls: **In the early 1950s, chief television producer Worthington Miner used popular CBS television theatre** *Studio One* **at times for repeating former Broadway hits. In one, Mr. Miner was fortunate in securing the rights to Robert E. Sherwood's play "Abe Lincoln in Illinois," as well as casting its original star of stage and screen, Raymond Massey, in his leading role as Lincoln. The broadcast was announced some weeks ahead as a super production, in this case the play's last scene to include Lincoln's historic farewell from Springfield to Washington, DC, from the rear platform of a realistic railroad passenger car, surrounded by a huge group of Springfield, Illinois, citizens enthusiastically displaying their love for the famed lawyer. The evening arrived as millions of TV patrons throughout the nation were being entranced by a perfect presentation. The final scene became visible with the promised railroad car, surrounded by countless citizens/extras exuding their love for Honest Abe, adding to the noisy excitement as the railroad car magically, slowly appeared to be leaving the station. Stunningly, there was a breathless pause, after which a lone male voice called, "Goodbye, Mr. Massey!"**

Victor Jory (sinister bad guy in many productions): In the same interview mentioned earlier, Robbin continues, "Another science-fiction-related incident occurred on the *Tales of Tomorrow* broadcast of 'The Universal Solvant.' Victor Jory was a scientist living in a rooming house, who in his room was busy devising a liquid that would dissolve everything except its container. The next door roomer was a young lady that the Jory character was interested in. One day he succeeded in his quest, and set about devising a dramatic experiment to impress the young lady — and the TV audience. He got a huge round glass tub about 3 feet across and several feet high. He filled this with his magic fluid, water, and invited the girl next door to come and see and be impressed. The tub was rigged with hoses and pumps at the bottom. When Jory threw things into the tub, the camera would close in to show the things hidden by rising bubbles. Then we would cut away to Jory trying to make time with the girl, while stagehands rushed in and removed all the stuff. Then a cut back to the tub would reveal it to be empty except for a few gentle bubbles rising. All went well during dress rehearsal. But Jory was getting a bit interested himself in the actress playing the next door roomer, or else he got carried away by his part, because during the broadcast he tossed everything he could lift into the tub. The stage hands managed to get the tub clear while the camera was on Jory and the girl, but when we cut back, it turned out Jory had thrown the stuff into the tub with such force that it dislodged the hoses and pumps and they came floating up, bubbling away in a beautiful close-up shot! I can't remember what happened after that, but we finished the show somehow. I suppose we forged ahead as if nothing were wrong…but I do remember all went home laughing!"

Paul Newman (leading man of film): In the *U. S. Steel Hour*'s 1956 classic, "Bang the Drum Slowly," Paul Newman plays the pitcher Henry Wiggen and Albert Salmi played his on-the-road roommate, Bruce Pierson, a not-as-talented catcher on the same team. It was the opening scene, right after Wiggen's introduction. The team was on the road and the two men were sharing a hotel room. Wiggen was writing a letter, then wadded it up and tossed it to the trashcan — only to miss. "Some pitcher," Newman cleverly ad-libbed. "I can't even hit a wastebasket!"

In the same broadcast, a cast member was to fire a gun. It just clicked. The actor said gamely, "One more time," and tried again. This time it went off, to everyone's relief.

Sid Caesar: Mr. Caesar wrote two autobiographies, both of which describe a wealth of bloopers. One of the most memorable was when he was portraying an opera singer at the make-up table. All went well during the rehearsal, but when it was being broadcast for all to see, his brush slipped and resulted in a dark line on his cheek. Being the master of improvisation, Caesar just continued making more lines until there were two horizontal and two vertical, then he proceeded to play tic-tac-toe. This delighted the audience.

Another episode's goof is only funny in hindsight:

One of the features on *Your Show of Shows* was the "four Britishers," made up of Caesar and his regulars Carl Reiner, Imogene Coca, and Howard Morris. They would sit in a row, completely composed, no matter what went on around them. In this particular sketch, they were visited by a chimp. During rehearsal, the little fellow was wonderful — walking and jumping on them, fiddling with the men's ties, and, funniest of all, taking the shawl off of Coca and bundling himself up in it. After dinner, it was show time. Everyone was in place, and the camera's light came on. Tummy full now, Mr. Chimp was content to just sit beside them with the same air of calm as the humans.

One of the most hilarious bloopers on *Caesar's Hour* was unnoticed by the audience. Caesar was the eloquent attorney whose job it was to convince the jury that his client, played by Howard Morris, was innocent. So engrossed was the head juror in the heartrending speech that he blurted out "Not guilty." That's not what he was supposed to say! How did Caesar save the skit? By responding "What do you mean 'not guilty'? This little rat is *not guilty*?" and proceeding to tell the jury in great detail why they should convict him.

Is Sid Caesar not a genius?

Kate Smith, a gracious hostess

Kate Smith (singer and hostess): On her series, Kate Smith was a charming and engaging hostess, and we got the feeling she was talking to us personally. That's why it seemed so fitting that, when something went wrong on the show, she would say so.

On her December 29, 1953, broadcast, a musical trio called The Three Sons, whose instruments were an organ, an accordion, and a guitar, came on to do their act. The guitar and accordion were just fine, but the organ's electrical connection wasn't working. At first, the accordionist was winging it alone, then looked over at Kate and admitted the problem. She told the audience that their technicians would work on that and they'd get back to The Three Sons later. The next act was the wonderful black comedy team of Howell and Radcliff. A few minutes into their act, they saw that the other group's organ was now fixed and involved The Three Sons in the scene. The blending of the two acts was magical. Once Howell and Radcliff were finished and took their bows, Kate Smith re-introduced The Three Sons, who then did their musical numbers with gusto. One thing that was so impressive is that the accordionist played a piano during one song, with the bulky accordion still strapped onto his chest. Not an easy task!

Captain Video and the Video Rangers (children's show): Wright appeared on this series and recalls the following: **Doing a stint on *Captain Video and the Video Rangers* is a two-week, twelve-day contract show. There was, naturally, a good deal of memory work involved. There were situations where it was possible to conceal a script - for instance, under paperwork while at a desk or at the instrument panel of a space jeep. So this day, when seated at the controls of the space jeep, I neatly placed the scene's script out of camera sight before me on the instrument panel. There we were on the airwaves, speeding through space in search of the enemy while I was exchanging dialog with my fellow video ranger, standing behind me, when suddenly, he stopped mid speech. Forgetting his lines, he stammered "The map, the map!" he spoke. "Give me the map" as he reached over my shoulder, sweeping up my concealed script in his hand while the SOB, pretending to study the pages, continued the dialog as I desperately improvised my part in the scene. I forgot how I got even with him, but I did.**

Alan Young (comedian, co-star of *Mr. Ed*): In Young's book *Mister Ed and Me*, he describes a doozie of a blooper in a delightfully entertaining way. He said that he was to play the part of a wild-animal trainer who would come to the stage on a camel. He was then to get off the camel and be met by his bulldog assistant, who would deliver to him his whip and whistle. An elephant would be next to enter and she'd stand on her front legs. Young would then lead a sleek black panther out on a leash, and the panther would walk around and around him, getting him tangled in his leash. Young would bend over to pat him when a tiger would come out and bite him on the derriere.

Alan Young

(The tiger was actually harmless. Blind, he would gently latch onto the wallet in the back pocket of his trainer and be led to wherever he needed to go.) That was the comedy sketch, and all went quite well during rehearsals with the trainers nearby.

During the actual broadcast, however, the trainers were off-camera, so didn't have as much control over the animals as they normally would have. Thus, the aired show didn't go as anticipated.

When Young rode in on the camel, the applause from the audience startled the camel, who then lost control of his bladder. The bulldog slid on the now-wet stage, gulped down the whistle, let go of the whip, and ran to the side of the stage, where he stayed. The panther abandoned the idea of walking around Young and, instead, walked around the camera, scaled the curtain, and urinated on the boom operator. The elephant came in early and stood on Young's feet instead of her own front legs. When the audience roared with laughter, she lost control of her bowels! As Young said, "Our stage looked as though Noah's ark had made a pit stop." The panther, still on a leash, tore off the stage and up the aisle, dragging Young with him. The tiger came in as planned, but couldn't find Young, so he grabbed the first back pocket he could find — that of one of the cameramen, who then ran off. As Young concludes, "Our director closed the curtain, cued the orchestra and left — presumably for the real-estate business."

Despite this experience, thank goodness Mr. Young would not be averse to co-starring with an exceptional animal on *Mister Ed* years later.

Johns Hopkins Science Review: One of their shows of 1951 dealt with the question "Which came first, the chicken or the egg?" As a visual aid, they had put a rooster and a hen into a cage, and now the camera had panned over to the two, who were busy making whoopee!

Another of their episodes was about personal cleansers. Water would be available during broadcast, but wasn't there before then. During rehearsals, four women went through the motions of lathering up their hair, and all seemed well. Come time for the actual broadcast, the water was there all right. It was all over the place! The shampoo and hair had clogged the washbasins, which then overflowed while the ladies' hair was still sudsy.

The producers thought "Fear" would be a good subject for study. A female volunteer was attached to various paraphernalia to measure her vital signs, and the psychologist produced a king snake and tossed it at her. She reacted the way she was supposed to, but the snake didn't — he had bitten the psychologist.

Okay then, how about teaching the television audience about the effects of an atomic chain reaction? One hundred overlapping mousetraps were set up in a square formation with a sugar cube on each one. When an additional cube was thrown at the first one, it would cause the desired chain reaction. It worked – a few minutes <u>before</u> air time when the set-up was accidentally bumped by a crew member. "If you have never tried to set 100 mouse traps baited with sugar lumps in 10 minutes, you can't imagine the pace of activity that followed," recalled Lynn Poole.

Isn't science wonderful?

Bob Keeshan (star of *Captain Kangaroo*): Both of Keeshan's bloopers prove the old adage that one should avoid working on screen with animals or children.

A guest on his show one day was a mountain lion named Cougie. Animal trainer Ruth Manecke had instructed Keeshan never to turn his back to the cougar, but when he sat down on the Treasure House steps with him, he forgot. In response, Cougie leapt onto him and mischievously tried to pull the Captain's wig off his head.

Another day brought two Dachshunds to the show. They had a terrific act in which one dog would pounce on a seesaw, making a rubber frankfurter fly through the air, and the other dog would catch it in his mouth. It *seemed* like a sure kid pleaser. On the air, however, the second dog decided he didn't want a hotdog that day. Each time it came hurling through the air at him, he ducked.

Bill Cullen (ageless game-show host): This man has got to have been one of the best game-show hosts ever. His keen sense of humor and the mischievous sparkle in his eyes lit up the set. He was hosting one of the early, live episodes of *The Price is Right* when the prize being bid on was a day at the circus, with a live elephant serving as the symbol of the big event. As the camera caught sight of it, the animal was defecating on stage. How did Cullen handle it? By joking "Join us again on Monday when we'll have equal time for the Democratic party."

Bill Cullen, host of the original *The Price is Right*

Perry Como (singer extraordinaire): Director Kenneth Whelan's three-year-old daughter Susan appeared with Como on his show, per the star's request. She was to be with him while he sang "Did Your Mother Come From Ireland?" to her. All went well during rehearsal, but once it was being aired, she got the hiccups. Como lost his place in his song, but that was okay. He stopped, got a glass of water, told her to drink slowly and count to ten, and helped her get over her hiccups in his typically relaxed manner. It took three minutes. Once they were gone, he finished his song and got an ovation from a very appreciative studio audience.

Merv Griffin (singer, game-show host, creator, producer, and author): One of Griffin's earliest series was *The Hazel Bishop Show*, named, of course, for its sponsor. He was not only a singer on the show, but also helped with the commercials, as was common in that era. In this particular one, a young lady was to kiss him as he was singing, then he was to wipe the lipstick off with his handkerchief, after which he would show the clean hankie to the camera and say "No lipstick smears!" All went as planned during rehearsals. Now the show was on the air, Griffin was singing, and the lady kissed him. Unfortunately, the powerfully-hot lights caused some of his own makeup to rub off onto the hankie, causing a sizable, greasy stain. He quickly turned the handkerchief around so only the white portion showed, said his line, then quickly stuffed it into his pocket. The audience howled with laughter.

Don Knotts (co-star of *The Andy Griffith Show*): Believe it or not, lovable Don Knotts was a regular on a soap opera from 1953 to 1955! It was the long-running *Search For Tomorrow*, which was then airing for just fifteen minutes a day. It seems Knotts was typecast early in his career. He played Wilbur Peterson, who was too timid to speak to anyone but his sister. In one episode, he and Les Damon were in a scene in which Damon was giving him the riot act when suddenly he went up on his lines. Knotts' role required him to be mute during this scene, so he couldn't help his cast mate. Feeling there was no alternative, Damon stopped and asked the floor manager for his next line. Only one camera was to be working on that scene, but a second one was hurriedly brought in so it could be trained on Knotts while the other actor received his line.

That would never happen to Don Knotts. Or so he thought. On *The Steve Allen Show*, the use of TelePrompTers was offered to each cast member, but Knotts felt he didn't need it for a monologue he himself had written about a political candidate talking to his workers. Wrong! It began smoothly enough and he was getting some good laughs. Then he suddenly went blank. It was the most horrifying experience of his whole career. He ad-libbed a bit, and then the next line suddenly came to him. The rest of the skit went well, and the audience didn't realize anything had been amiss.

The Howdy Doody Show: This show was the model for children's shows to follow, but it did have its less-than-stellar moments. When one of the kids in the Peanut Gallery needed to go to the bathroom, he didn't leave the set and go backstage. Instead, he just did his business in a nearby pumpkin.

Man Against Crime: In this detective show, the main character had all suspects in a hospital room for the confrontation. Then he forgot his lines. After a few awkward moments, the supposedly mute (due to bandages covering his head) patient fed him his lines. The viewers heard both men!

James Cagney (tough-guy cinema star): This was probably the only live television show Cagney had ever done. It was a 1956 *Robert Montgomery*

Presents episode entitled "Soldier from the Wars Returning." He had a very long monologue about the meaning of life. Two pages long. He did beautifully until its climax, when his mind suddenly went blank. While waiting for Cagney to regain his bearings, they shot from various camera angles, close-ups and farther back. Finally, the line came to the actor and the show ended as planned. It was quite a surprise the next day to discover that the critics were raving about the production and especially its long monologue! "James Cagney could teach all these new-fangled television actors a thing or two about the value of silence," one column read. "Not unlike Beethoven's Fifth, with a pause at the end of the first four notes…"

Steven Marlo (prolific television guest star): The biggest blooper that Steven Marlo recalls in live TV was a painful one. "In dress rehearsal, I'm supposed to say a line and turn to the right. I don't know what the hell the cameraman was doing. As I turned to the right, he didn't pull back, and I walked right into the lens and broke my nose!" They thought at first that they would have to cancel the play, but Marlo refused to give up. "They took me to the emergency hospital that tried to refix the nose. I was up all night with cold compresses to keep the swelling down, but I still got through the show."

Steven Marlo

Helen Wagner (veteran star of daytime drama): Helen Wagner, of *As The World Turns*, told radio interviewer Peter Anthony Holder about this blooper: "When you're on the air you don't have the stove connected, because a hot stove is too much of a danger in that kind of situation. One day we did have it [connected] because they decided that they wanted to see Nancy frying chicken for the 4th of July picnic. So I was frying chicken for the 4th of July picnic and, in the midst of everything, one of the timers on the stove went off. Well, we had never used the stove before. None of us had any idea where the timer was. We were playing a sort of laissez faire attitude toward this old thing and, meanwhile, one of the stagehands was crawling behind the set, pulling the plug on the stove. You know the great cook Nancy didn't even know how her stove worked."

Ed Sullivan (*Toast of the Town* host): Working on Ed Sullivan's show was a challenge sometimes. Sullivan would be changing elements of it almost up to the last moment before going on the air. Once a substitute floor manager was getting acts in place while the show was on the air, but he had not been advised of the latest changes. Sullivan gave a long, elaborate introduction to Peggy Lee, but when the curtain parted, it was a trapeze act on stage.

The Garry Moore Show: The audio was just fine when the ventriloquist spoke, but the audience couldn't hear the dummy's lines. Why? The inexperienced man on the mike boom was moving the mike back and forth instead of keeping it on the ventriloquist!

Lucy and Desi (one of the most beloved comedy teams in television history): Okay, okay. Technically, *I Love Lucy* was not broadcast live. The pilot was, but not the series. Still, though, it filmed live before an audience and rarely required a retake, so it had many of the fun and nerve-wracking aspects of live television. If a mistake was made, they usually just kept right on acting and it was broadcast that way. Now, with the season-by-season release of the show on DVD, we get to see those delicious bloopers again.

In "Lucy Makes a Commercial," one of the series' classic episodes, Lucille Ball inadvertently skipped a couple lines of the spiel after having imbibed many spoonsful of the potent product. Staying perfectly in character, she remembered the missing lines, went back, and slurringly said them with a flourish, making the show even funnier than it was written. "She did it so smoothly, even I didn't notice," says her writer Madelyn Pugh Davis.

In the episode "Cuban Pals," Ricky was translating for Lucy and his Cuban friends — from Spanish-to-English for Lucy, and from English-to-Spanish for his friends. Once, however, he tells the Cubans, "Lucy wants to know if you had a...", catches himself with an "Oh, fine!", then, while trying not to laugh at his gaffe, said the line in Spanish, as it was intended. At least, when that happened, we realized he was truly translating, rather than just making it *sound* as if he were. Not surprising, really, considering Spanish was Desi Arnaz's native tongue.

And how about the great Harpo's appearance on the classic 1955 episode "Lucy and Harpo Marx" in which he and Lucy did the famous mirror scene? After catching Lucy's friend Carolyn Appleby, played by Doris Singleton, he draped her over his shoulder and was carrying her out of the room when his hat fell off. He was still carrying her, but stooped to pick up his hat, then made his exit through the door with woman in tow. This would be pretty amazing for any man, but Harpo was sixty-seven years old at the time and had a serious heart condition! A thorough professional.

CHAPTER TEN

THE AUDIENCE

The most important part of live television to an actor was the audience. What did your viewers then and now (in retrospect) tell you, Wright?

Reactions to television performances presented a problem to most all of us in live television. The earliest reactions came, of course, from our families, friends, and neighbors. With the few newly-appointed newspaper and magazine critics — never the next day as most of us in theatre had become accustomed to reading — but later in the week.

Says Jack Klugman, "You'd finish at 9:00 or 10:00 and you'd go home. You'd go out on the street, and they'd say 'I just saw you' and 'You were wonderful' or 'You were bad.' You learned a lot. I learned a great deal."

The day after "Marty" aired, Rod Steiger was greeted on the street by friends and strangers alike by his character's name. The show had made a huge impact on them.

Sometimes a fan letter slipped through and maybe a director would let you know of a happy result. The best way was my agent's phone ringing in my behalf.

Wondering what live television was like for the average viewers, we asked them. Here's what they said:

Oklahoma resident Pamela Greenwood was a member of the audience during an early live broadcast of *The Red Skelton Show*. Having seen many different programs, she was quite impressed that Skelton would do the pre-show warm-up himself, expressing profound gratitude to his audience for their support. Another thing that probably endeared Skelton to the audience is the fact that he had high standards, refusing to

Lovable Red Skelton in a project with child star Margaret O'Brien

resort to off-color humor. He had too much respect for his audience and the art of comedy to do that.

On the other shows Greenwood visited, she learned that when Jack Paar's talk show was in commercial, Paar's attention was diverted from the guest by his makeup artist, director, and others. It was when the camera was on them again that he was able to refocus on the show's guest. Another thing that she remembers is the "Applause" sign stage hands would hold up to cue the audience.

Emily Peters of Brooklyn has vivid memories of early television. "When I hear the term 'live TV'," she says, "the first thing that comes to mind is Milton Berle, as his was the first live TV show I ever saw. Most families in our neighborhood didn't own a set and we'd gather in front of the appliance store on Tuesday nights and watch Milton Berle through the window on the screen that was probably not more than ten inches." She continues, "I particularly enjoyed the drama programs like *Studio One* and *The Alcoa Hour*, and recall that many actors who later became big stars started out in those shows. I also remember that, because the shows were live, there were always errors with usually hilarious results, such as a supposed dead body getting up and walking off camera. Most of all, I remember the Dave Garroway early morning show that was the forerunner of the current *Today* show. I think it was his idea to have the studio at street level at NBC so that people could watch through the window. Maybe it's just my nostalgia talking, but I think, with the exception of Johnny Carson, that these early innovators of TV programming have no present-day equal in talent, intelligence and, above all, graciousness, and never had to rely on vulgarities, insults or compulsive talking for attention."

Pittsburgh resident Janet Marburger was watching many of the same things. She says, "My parents and I used to visit a few neighbors who were the first owners of TVs in our town in the early 50s. The first show that comes to mind is Milton Berle (Uncle Milty) and his sponsor, Texaco. There was also Sid Caesar and Imogene Coca…they were funny. I remember we were so enthralled with the TV screen that we even thought the commercials were great. We were also inclined to applaud performers until we realized how silly that was." Vivid in her husband Roy's memory are the 1952 Democratic and Republican conventions. "It was a shambles because they washed all their dirty linen in front of the audience, which turned out to be quite embarrassing. They didn't have TV savvy at that point in time."

Paul Goldsmith, of Brooklyn, was a regular viewer of *Watch Mr. Wizard*. He felt it was a very clever approach to include a child in the scientific experiments because identifying with the child alleviated any intimidation a child viewer might have had. The guest-child was learning, just as the viewer-child was. Goldsmith went on to teach electronics in a vocational school and has maintained an interest in physics throughout his life. He feels that *Watch Mr. Wizard* helped its audience develop analytical thinking.

Lawton, Oklahoma resident Michael George recalls a very special day in June, 1954. He accompanied his little six- and eight-year-old sisters to an airing of *Howdy Doody* and sat with them in the Peanut Gallery. The show was broadcast from Radio City Music Hall in New York City. All seemed to go as he expected, except for one little thing. It was somewhat strange to see Clarabell, off-stage but in costume, talking!

Buffalo Bob, Clarabell, and Howdy Doody

Rev. Marguerite Oetjen lives in Estonia now, but she grew up in the United States and was watching TV just like the rest of us back in the good old days. Here's what she remembers: "We didn't have TV, so yes, I watched with neighbors. I had an aunt who had been a dancer in earlier years and had a ballet school in Boston. One of her pupils, Nanci Crompton, occasionally appeared on Ed Sullivan, so we always made arrangements to see those shows and catch her brief appearances on Sunday nights. Of course, the other Sunday night show was Steve Allen, with its brilliant host and its wonderful characters. Why do I remember his 'breaking up' in the midst of a sketch? I guess it made him very authentic — as if he hadn't memorized lines someone else had written.

"We must have come into a TV somewhere in the mid-50's, because I do remember the wonderful dramas on *Studio One* when I was in high school. Somehow, I think the black-and-white added to the power of those shows. And, oddly, I still have a fairly vivid memory of a single show — watching Lee Ann Meriwether winning the *long* Miss America contest in 1955. I picked her to win early in the pageant, was very impressed with her dramatic reading, and 'rooted for her' during the rest of the unfolding 'drama.' I recall being pleased that she appeared in other shows after her 'reign.'

"I also remember my mother, a devout Catholic, watching 'Uncle Fulty'— which was how Bishop Fulton Sheen was referred to in jest — in competition with 'Uncle Milty' Berle. The Bishop didn't mind — he had a sense of humor! (In retrospect, isn't it almost unbelievable that there could have been a Bishop in prime time TV on a major network?!)"

Writer S. L. Kotar remembers the "TV sets built into magnificent cabinets which was a huge piece of furniture all by itself. Even with doors to close over the screen when you weren't watching it!"

Kotar recalls hearing Richard Kiley talking about a very special show: "He said if a show were really popular they would try and bring back the cast in the next few days and stage it again. That's how we got 'Patterns' – it was a Rod Serling teleplay and was so popular when they first performed it, they got the cast back and did it again. Those were the days when you could get all sorts of people in a production. This one had Ed Begley, Richard [Kiley], Elizabeth Montgomery (in a very small role) and other actors. What a wonderful time!" This took place in 1955 (January 12th and February 9th) on the *Kraft Television Theatre*.

Virginia music director Jacqueline Bitler remembers most the commercials of her childhood. "TV certainly was a novelty then," she says of the time spent in front of her neighbor's television set. "I guess this would make the merchandisers happy, but I sure remember a lot of early commercials. The jingles were so brazen and in-your face ("Brusha, brusha, brusha. Use the new Ipana;" "Get the best, get Sealtest;" "See the USA in your Chevrolet.") Nothing like the esoteric ads we see today, where I sometimes don't know what they're selling."

New Yorker Ted Pilonero misses the values of live TV. Among his favorites from that time was *Lassie*, "which was a bit sappy, but had real-life stories about real people with solid values, something which is about impossible to find on TV today. I loved *Gunsmoke*, which also was real stories about people with strong values and guiding principles…

"Also, the variety shows, like Ed Sullivan's [first known as *Toast of the Town*, then renamed in 1955 to *The Ed Sullivan Show*]…were quite entertaining, and a real variety. There was none of the recent competitive drivel to be the best singer, dancer or comedian…But today's multitude of shows seemingly has diluted the number of viewers on any single show/channel, so low-cost production with a lot of ads seems to be where we 'progressed' to."

"The early days of TV were much better than today," agrees Jack Lambert from North Carolina. "*Howdy Doody* with Buffalo Bob, Sheri Lewis and Lambchop, *The Ed Sulllivan Show*, Milton Berle, Jack Benny – the variety of entertainment was real because it was live with no editing out of mistakes, and I think that was where some of the most funny and interesting times came from. Ed Sullivan had guests on that the average person would never be able to see otherwise…TV was family driven, and I watched it with my mom and dad at home…on one black-and-white TV. But we watched it <u>together</u> in the same room as a family, not as they do today with a TV in every room."

That's a very important point. The average family, if they had a television set at all, had only one, and it would usually be in the living room. The family would gather around and watch it together. A show's content would often be the topic of conversation for them afterward. Thus, television united people and stimulated conversation — just the opposite of today.

Lambert continues, "It seems that a lot of the early TV shows came from the Golden Age of Radio. It was a transition for the stars. We knew them by sound, and now we could see them as well."

* * *

Ask any actor who has been prominent on the TV screen over the years and most will agree that it isn't unusual to be approached almost anywhere by fans, strangers who are curious about meeting you in person or even being complimentary about your talent. Admittedly, for me these days, it is not an everyday occurrence, but it's a good feeling when it happens. It reminds me of a meeting over a year ago that you might find interesting. My wife June and I were taking a cross-country trip by car, and after an entire day of Texas freeway, we were checking into a hotel in Texas. A friendly stranger approached me with a happy, knowing smile, craftily inquiring, "Wheeeere have I seen you?" Returning his knowing smile, I stated, "Well, I've been in some motion pictures and a lot of television." His smile was replaced with a serious stare as he announced, "I passed you three times on the freeway today."

CHAPTER ELEVEN

MEMORABLE PEOPLE OF THE LIVE TV ERA

Wright, you've worked with the greatest that New York and Hollywood had to offer. Who do you remember most fondly from the live-television era?

Two men I admire are producers/directors WORTHINGTON MINER (of *Studio One*) and FRED COE (of *Philco Playhouse*). They each had their areas of expertise and, between them, shaped television, making it what it is today.

According to *The Man in the Shadows: Fred Coe and the Golden Age of Television*, by Jon Krampner, Yale instructor Otto Preminger had a high regard for Coe, too. His forte was bringing out the best in his performers as a director and, likewise, bringing out the best in his writers as a producer. He treated them with respect and made corrections gently. The great Delbert Mann learned his directorial craft from Coe. When the two men were guiding the Town Theatre in Columbia, South Carolina, that was its most successful time, according to actress Jo Brown.

Fred Coe

Coe had a tender heart, too. During the dark days of McCarthyism and black lists, Coe did what he could to give work to writers and actors who were considered controversial. The advertisers, who were usually extremely timid about breaking rules, wouldn't know about it until it was on the air. Coe seemed to subscribe to the philosophy that "forgiveness is easier to get than permission." In the live-TV environment, which was fast-paced and stressful, Coe was calm and very deliberate.

Many people have expressed similar admiration for Fred Coe. Director Arthur Penn felt Coe had no equal in television.

In June, 1954, I was privileged to appear in *Philco TV Playhouse*'s "The Shadow of Willie Greer," which was produced by Fred Coe and written by

Horton Foote

Yul Brynner

Harry Townes

Phillip Pine

another great man, HORTON FOOTE. There were so many excellent producers and directors in early TV. STANLEY QUINN, SIDNEY LUMET, MAURY HOLLAND, PAUL NICKELL, and ROBERT STEVENS come to mind, too, in this context. Sidney Lumet was my very favorite director.

Being directed by YUL BRYNNER in *Studio One* and *Starlight Theatre* was a real treat. He was a very genial man, and was so excited to finally have a directing job after being an actor for a number of years. Did you know he had been an acrobat in Europe before becoming an actor? He was a fascinating person, and so easy and nice to work with.

Director Ted Post, too, was quite fond of Brynner because he was generous with his time in helping Post when he was new to directing.

HARRY TOWNES, a friend over the many years since our live TV days. Harry and I, working on *Studio One*, discovered we lived within blocks of each other on Long Island. Then some time later June, our boys, and I moved to Los Angeles, settling down in the San Fernando Valley. We'd been there a short time before we discovered Harry had settled down two blocks from us there, too! We, coincidentally, were in a number of TV shows out there and took turns driving to work. Actor PHILIP PINE and Harry and I were all close friends (incidentally, from two different Claire Tre Major Children's Theatre tours, way back there). Phil had the lead on one of the early live TV theatre soap operas. The producers of that soap opera decided to do some recasting, and Phil was obliged to show up and audition for the same role! MARION DOUGHERTY, a uniquely talented casting director, had a lot to do with my success, as well as others, in casting for live television. JOE SCULLY and ELINOR KILGALLEN helped greatly in putting us together in the Golden Years with Hollywood greats, the likes of Melvyn Douglass, Lucille Ball, and Yul Brynner.

And, on the subject of Brynner — we've spoken of him earlier about his enthusiasm for directing. Just as he embarked on the beginning of adding direction to his acting career, he was faced with the decision of playing a lead role in an up-and-coming musical or joining the group of live television directors. He confided that it was going to be arranged for him to do both. Who could have predicted his overwhelming success in the Rodgers and Hammerstein *The King and I* musical hit? It was pretty clear that options of direction were not to be a part of his near future. There's bittersweet in success, too.

Marion Dougherty

Back to the Golden Years and a golden girl — MARIA RIVA, a talented young actress, undiscovered until the Golden Age, went straight to the hearts of remote screens across the country. I spent some good times with her on several TV shows, trading stories of our interesting mothers and happy families. We both just kept having sons. Biographies are my favorite kind of reading, and Maria wrote one of the finest, attested the critics.

Maria Riva

Actors are great friends and among them was a cute gal, very young, just, I'm sure, still in, or maybe just out of high school, with lots of acting ability. Once, during a rehearsal break from a *Kraft Television Theatre* show, we were conversing at lunch in a midtown restaurant. She paused for a short time, studying life on the street outside her window, and, turning to me, LEE REMICK simply announced, "There's a broken heart for every light on Broadway." Now who would'a thought?

Lee Remick

After ten years of marriage and their two careers, DESI ARNAZ and LUCILLE BALL decided to form their own act. Ken Murray booked them on his New York-based television variety show as a kind of tryout. I felt fortunate to be a part of that production and, not long afterward, I was not surprised to learn that their act had paved the way to their smash *I Love Lucy*.

Those are wonderful memories, Wright.

There was another woman who really made a mark for herself. Just as Raymond Massey was called on multiple times to portray Abe Lincoln, so was **Kim Stanley** repeatedly cast as Joan of Arc. One of the live stage's greatest actresses, she had just the qualities needed to bring that strong, pious character to life. She lent her talents not only to the Broadway stage, but also to live television. *You Are There* cast her in their 1953 presentation of "The Final Hours of Joan of Arc."

Let's see whom other actors and actresses remember the most:

Comedian Sid Caesar was pleasantly surprised to discover, during **Charlton Heston's** guest appearances on his shows, that he was an excellent straight man. If the leading-man business ever dried up, Heston now had a second career to fall back on.

Another of Caesar's favorites was **Hugh Downs**. "He was the most elegant of all announcers," he said at the Museum of Broadcasting Seminar Series.

In his autobiographical *Mister Ed and Me*, Alan Young expresses his deep admiration for **Ed Wynn's** innovativeness and wisdom. Young would listen intently to his encouraging words of advice, words that would still be with him decades later.

Jimmy Durante's kindness and generosity is fondly remembered by him as well.

Singer/actor Bill Hayes has a lot of respect for **Sid Caesar:** "He was a very physical performer, which set him apart from the radio comedians who were moving into television. And Sid had that rare musician's ear for the lilt of languages other than American English, plus the ability to replicate them in total gibberish. His imagination was so strong and his body control so complete he only had to think a pantomimic situation and his hands and physique would perform it."

Hayes continues, "The writers would tell him who he was, in what situation, and Sid would flip the switch and out would come reality and truth, heightened just enough to be funny. To me, Sid's work on *Your Show of Shows* was the peak of his powers. There wasn't a thing he couldn't do — except maybe tell a joke. I never heard him tell a joke onstage or off. His comedy was a vein of gold that came out of the ore of life."

Rance Howard remembers most his director on *Kraft Television Theatre*, **William Graham,** who also directed him almost twenty years later in the 1974 film *When Lilies Bloom*. The players he remembers fondly from those days are **Jack Klugman, Albert Salmi,** and **Betsy Von Furstenberg.** Howard has a very long list of credits, but he treasures the experiences he had on that show.

Bob Keeshan, known by several generations as Captain Kangaroo, felt that the master of live television was **Bob Smith,** otherwise known as Buffalo

Bob of *Howdy Doody* fame. He learned so much from him during his stint as Clarabell.

Actress Claire Kirby Hooton has the highest regard for off-camera people. "My strongest memory is of the directors," she says, "particularly **Arthur Penn,** who practically got inside me to orchestrate his direction. He was very respectful of method-trained actors and would hush the other actors around the set while you were quietly preparing the scene. A good guy."

Legendary actor James Dean was in awe of much-older **Walter Hampton.** At first, Dean had been disrespectful but, once he saw what a truly great actor he was, his attitude changed completely and he treated him as royalty.

Director Kenneth Whelan admires most **Noel Coward,** who was very professional, cooperative, and respectful; and **Helen Hayes,** who was gracious and wonderfully diplomatic. Whelan's directorial ideas weren't working, but Hayes blamed herself and asked his permission to try another way. That saved not only the show, but also his pride. She was a true lady.

Whelan also worked with **Dick Van Dyke** on *The Morning Show*. In an industry that is noted for its eccentricities, Van Dyke was refreshingly normal and his morals were admirable. Humor came naturally to him.

Betsy Palmer worked with **James Dean** in both *Studio One* and *Danger*, and they were romantically involved. What was he like? "Exactly the way he came across — spooky," she says. "We got together because we were both from Indiana. We were just two kids. We liked to talk about acting, and our approach to it was sort of the same way. He had a great look for when he was the rebel because he *was* a rebel without a cause."

Another co-star who was memorable to her was **Tyrone Power.** "He was a darling. A sweet, sweet man."

Peter Mark Richman has a high regard for director **Arthur Penn.** "Arthur Penn was a very hot television director in those days, and he went on to do *Bonnie and Clyde* in films. He's a terrific director and one of the leading directors of live television. He's a wonderful guy."

Another of Richman's fond memories is of **Ann Harding.** "I remember she was a lovely lady and a very prepared character woman. Good actress. And she used to have a little case that you could carry. She would make a drink of gelatin and water with juice during the rehearsal. She just drank those things and didn't take any adulterated food."

Ed Begley, Sr., is another of Richman's favorites. "Wonderful character actor, Ed Begley. You've seen him a hundred times. I've worked with him many times…You can't ever deny what a great personality he was.

Steven Marlo adored working with **Lucille Ball.** "She was my favorite of all," he says. "I love Lucille Ball."

His favorite live-TV director was **George Fenady.** He and his brother **Andrew,** who directed movies, were both excellent, Marlo feels.

Jack Klugman's very favorite director was **Bob Mulligan.** Director **Sidney Lumet** has a special place in his heart, as well. "Directors then came from

Left: Lucille Ball was much loved
Right: Tony Randall, who was a regular on many successful series over the years.

the theatre," he says. "They were overqualified for television. They knew how to use rehearsal."

Klugman also had a huge respect for producer **Fred Coe.** "He was a genius! One of only a few geniuses I knew. He would come in on Friday and give you notes. He watched the performance (of *Philco Television Playhouse* and *Producers' Showcase* productions) and give you notes, and the notes were so specific and so good. He was really wonderful."

Others, too, served to make live television great. "Look at who came out of it. My God! The writers, the directors, the actors. **Eli Wallach, Paul Newman, Jimmy Dean** — they all came from television."

In his book, *Tony and Me,* Klugman indicates another person who made an impression on him in the early 1950s. He used to watch the live broadcasts of *Mr. Peepers,* and that was the first time he ever set eyes on **Tony Randall,** a regular on that show. Klugman says he became an instant fan. Randall's acting was so honest and so perfectly-executed. Little did Klugman know then that in just a few years, he would be working with Randall on another live television show, *Appointment With Adventure* and, much later, they would become a very important team on *The Odd Couple*, as well as close friends.

On a *Playhouse 90*, Betsy Palmer was cast with **Jackie Gleason** in Saroyan's "The Time of Your Life." They had heard that Gleason was sometimes difficult to work with, so they hired Miss Palmer, too, in hopes that her calmness would keep him calm, or at least she wouldn't give them additional conflict. It turned out his reputation had apparently been exaggerated. "He was an absolute doll," she says, "a lovely man, and couldn't work hard enough or long enough. He was the best."

Betsy Palmer and Jackie Gleason on *Playhouse 90*

Director Kenneth Whelan, too, has a high regard for Gleason, and feels that his beginning years at CBS were his most creative. It seemed to stir up his juices to know that millions of people were watching. Gleason had an affection for unemployed actors and would be sure to have a crowd scene on his show a couple times a year so these actors could feel the adrenaline rush of stage work again.

(Jackie Gleason also starred in *Studio One*'s presentation of "The Laughmaker" in 1953. His own theme song that he wrote, "Melancholy Serenade," and his "Honeymooners" sidekick Art Carney were included in this show. How interesting it was to see the two men play such different parts — Gleason as a comedian whose suffers much rejection in his personal life, and Carney as a skeptical journalist.)

Don Grady's favorite people to work with in that era were Mouseketeers **Cubby, Karen, Annette** and **Darlene**. "They were great people! They still are." While *The Mickey Mouse Club* was filmed ahead of time, it was usually done in one take.

CHAPTER TWELVE

GOOD-BYE TO THE GOLDEN AGE

Videotape began being used with regularity in 1956.

According to the Museum of Broadcast Communions, Bing Crosby had been a pioneer in the taping business. It seems he wasn't fond of broadcasting his TV specials live, so his production company began using magnetic videotape in 1951. Desi Arnaz and Lucille Ball were trailblazers, too. They wanted to broadcast their show from their home state of California, but their sponsors, Philip Morris, felt there were more smokers in New York, so wanted it aired from the east coast. New York had been relying on kinescope — taking a movie of the television screen as the live show was being aired — but it had its limitations. *I Love Lucy*'s sponsor wouldn't accept the inferior picture quality of kinescope for its New York viewers, so Arnaz, with the help of cinematographer Karl Freund, put the show on film, using three cameras. Everyone was happy with the result.

You recall another way film was used on television, don't you, Wright?

With the breakup of the studio system and the mass exodus of big-name stars to the East Coast, Hollywood had to do something. Who should come up with a solution but Hopalong Cassidy himself, William Boyd. His many films had been run in the movie houses, then were stored away, where they were gathering dust. Boyd bought the films and made them available for showing on television. That idea opened up more possibilities. "Why can't New York shows be put on film?" Hollywood moguls wondered. And it happened. In the process, television began moving to California.

Hollywood did have better facilities, after all, which would give them more space for broadcasting. Space had been at a premium in crowded New York City. But filming and taping the shows gave acting a whole different feel.

"I remember them saying in the beginning, 'It's going to be just like live television, except we'll be able to see it immediately,'" recalls Betsy Palmer. "Well, we'd start the scene, and they'd say, 'Wait a minute! Stop, stop. Let's go back. Let's redo that.' It got to be totally different."

As Jack Klugman recalls, "When they went to California to make money, that was when television became terrible." New York City's focus had been quality. Hollywood seemed to have different values. "We used to do *Studio One* and *Playhouse 90* (in New York). We had a lot of rehearsal, and that's where the performance really grows. Johnny Frankenheimer once flooded the studio with water to do Faulkner's *Old Man*. It was a wonderful performance, but it almost ruined the studio, but he didn't care. The performance was the most important thing." (This episode was a *Playhouse 90* production, adapted for television by Horton Foote and starring Sterling Hayden and Geraldine Page. The story was about the Mississippi River flood.)

Indeed, since film made retakes an option, very little time was given for rehearsal now. What are your thoughts about this development, Wright?

At this time, the film directors began a disturbing "shoot the rehearsal" threat. For live television actors accustomed to adequate rehearsal in order to feel comfortable in their roles, to have the powers-that-be just shrug off the need for such preparation is unsettling. They feel that what's going to be shown to audiences is often less than their best.

"It's more like doing a movie," says Rance Howard. "You don't have time to rehearse and discover or develop the character the way you did on live TV when they were really doing things like *Kraft Television Theatre, Kaiser Aluminum Hour, U.S. Steel Hour, Studio One* — all those classic, great live dramas.

Betty Furness lamented, "The undoing of *Studio One* is when they moved to the west coast. Those of us who started in television in New York had a very dim view of Hollywood and thought that television belonged in New York. We were very proud of what had been accomplished here." The energy level went way down once they weren't working live anymore. No more nervous energy. Too, the people themselves changed when they moved to California. They got too relaxed because their work became too easy. There was no continuity on *Studio One* anymore, no central focus. It was no longer fun for her, but she waited until election night 1960 was over before quitting. She loved to work at political conventions and didn't want to miss this last one. Then she quit while talking on camera to news anchor Walter Cronkite. She told him it was the last time she would say goodnight, and walked out. By then, she was too associated with Westinghouse products to be a convincing journalist, so this was quite a gamble. All turned out well for her when she later got a job for consumerism that took her to the White House.

It seems that one very big reason live television was able to be so completely replaced by film is that the only way a live broadcast could be seen again (clearly, though, not on fuzzy kinescope) would be to perform it again. This was done sometimes, but it was so much easier and more cost effective to just record it on film, then reshow it later. The second airing of a recorded production would then be practically one hundred percent profit.

Ratings and profit became the goal now.

The atmosphere on the set of filmed TV is so different from that of live

TV. Gone now, for the most part, are the camaraderie, the enthusiasm, and the excitement. Bill Erwin says, "The sound stages of today are not as much fun as they used to be. Everything is dark on the stage except the scene being shot and very technical. No laughing or chit chat as of old."

Don Knotts had reservations about film, too. True, it gave him and his cast mates a sense of security and provided a more laid-back environment, but it seemed to him that the laugh track made the producers care less about the quality of the show's humor. "Don't worry about it. The laugh track will love it," he was told when a joke didn't seem particularly funny to him. He missed the excitement of live TV.

Bill Erwin now

When the ten-year-old *Studio One*, the ultimate in originality and professionalism, moved to Hollywood, it died.

So did the Golden Age.

What had begun as the age of experimentation was now the age of big business. Quiz shows fell to scandal when it became known that answers had been given before air time to the most popular contestants. Nothing seemed real anymore.

The anthologies of yesteryear required a thinking audience to be appreciated. Character analysis was often emphasized more than complicated plots. They were written in a very human way about experiences Americans could relate to. It was reality. Each production usually had a point to make. (An excellent example of this is Paul Newman's emotional closing line in *Bang the Drum Slowly*, "From here on in, I rag nobody!")

Later action programs, by contrast, were pure escapism. The audiences didn't have to think anymore.

Writer Paddy Chayefsky felt that live television dramatized ordinary lives and promoted understanding. Could the lack of that today have something to do with the different types of problems we have now — shootings in schools, instability of families, hate crimes, etc? There's a lack of empathy. Now it's all about profit and prestige, not art or understanding.

Wright, after pioneering in live television for the years before they went to Hollywood, then you spent much of your time making movies, how do you feel about that today?

In the very early 1950s it became apparent to many of us live TV-ers that the US television viewers out there were growing rapidly. Most

Paul Newman, Albert Salmi, and George Peppard in "Bang the Drum Slowly"
PHOTOFEST

entertainment was in demand and television recording would be in many ways an answer to our problems. While the kinescope was a TV recording, it was obviously a crude process and would soon be replaced by "tape", a viable recording process-in-the-works. Hollywood was certain that it had the answer to recording — film. And there was proof in William Boyd's presenting ancient recordings of his Hopalong Cassidy western films — the television reacted immediately by seeing them all over again on TV! Additionally, a new system developed by actor Desi Arnaz, together with cinematographer Karl Freund, for the showing of the famous *I Love Lucy* series. Lucy did not have to go east to do her show. Television went to her. It presented final proof.

All this together plus "tape", successful at last, was too late on the scene. No pun intended.

As for me personally…how do I feel about it today? I left New York finally in 1955 and joined the many fellow actors in the move to California, continuing in my chosen profession, always with the theatre in the long run at the top of my list.

It was a tough change in a way; acting in live television and acting before a motion picture camera had its problems, but Hollywood was very hospitable and I continued performing on both stages, theatre and sound. It's amazing to discover that most of my thirty years of performing were in television…What a life!!!!

Perhaps old is becoming new again. Some of the modern-day shows have taken to live broadcasting. Many of today's leading men and women got their start in stand-up comedy. Raymond Romano and Jerry Seinfeld performed their shows before live audiences, which made them extra special. The best teacher for an actor is a live audience, night after night, and these two men know that. And look at all the talented folks whose careers have been launched by *Saturday Night Live*, a show that has lasted over thirty years and won numerous awards.

There must be something to this new "live" concept!

BIBLIOGRAPHY

Books:

Arnaz, Desi, *A Book*. New York: William Morris and Company, Inc., 1976

Brooks, Tim and Marsh, Earle, *The Complete Directory to Prime Time Network TV Shows 1946-Present*. New York: Ballantine Books, 1979.

Caesar, Sid with Bill Davidson, *Where Have I Been? An Autobiography*. New York: Crown Publishers, Inc., 1982

Caesar, Sid with Eddy Friedfeld, *Caesar's Hours: My Life in Comedy, With Love and Laughter*. New York: Public Affairs, 2003.

Chambers, Stan, *News at Ten*. Santa Barbara: Capra Press, 1994.

Conniff, James C.G., *The Bishop Sheen Story*. New York: Fawcett Publications, Inc., 1953.

Dunn, Kate, *Do Not Adjust Your Set: The Early Days of Live Television*. London: John Murray (Publishers), 2003.

Geier, Leo, *Ten Years with Television at Johns Hopkins*. Baltimore: Johns Hopkins University, 1958.

Grabman, Sandra, *Spotlights & Shadows: The Albert Salmi Story*. Albany: BearManor Media, 2004.

Griffin, Merv with David Bender, *Merv: Making the Good Life Last*. New York: Simon & Schuster, 2003.

Hayes, Bill and Susan Seaforth Hayes, *Like Sands Through the Hourglass*. New York: New American Library, 2005.

Hutchinson, Tom, *Rod Steiger*. New York: Fromm International, 2000.

Keeshan, Bob, *Good Morning, Captain*. Minneapolis: Fairview Press, 1996.

Kindem, Gorham, *The Live Television Generation of Hollywood Film Directors*. Jefferson: McFarland & Company, Inc., Publishers, 1994.

Kisseloff, Jeff, *The Box: An Oral History of Television 1920-1961*. New York: Penguin Books, 1995.

Klugman, Jack with Burton Rocks, *Tony and Me: A Story of Friendship*. West Linn: Good Hill Press, 2005

Knotts, Don with Robert Metz, *Barney Fife and Other Characters I Have Known*. New York: Berkley Boulevard, 1999.

Krampner, Jon, *Female Brando: The Legend of Kim Stanley*. New York: Back Stage Books, 2006.

Krampner, Jon, *The Man in the Shadows: Fred Coe and the Golden Age of Television*. New Brunswick: Rutgers University Press, 1997.

MacDonald, J. Fred, *One Nation Under Television: The Rise and Decline of Network TV*. Chicago: Nelson-Hall Publishers, 1994.

Marx, Bill, *Son of Harpo Speaks!* Albany: BearManor Media, 2007

Morgan, Henry, *Here's Morgan!* New York: Barricade Books, Inc., 1994

Stashower, Daniel, *The Boy Genius and the Mogul*. New York: Broadway Books, 2002.

Whelan, Kenneth, *How the Golden Age of Television Turned My Hair to Silver*. New York: Walker and Company, 1973.

Wilk, Max, *Golden Age of Television: Notes from the Survivors*. New York: Moyer Bell Limited, 1989.

Young, Alan, *Mr. Ed and Me*. New York: St. Martin's Press, 1994.

Young, Alan, *There's No Business Like Show Business…Was*. Albany: BearManor Media, 2006.

Magazines:

Cohen, Harold V., "Stop, You're Killing Me!" *TV Digest*, Vol. X, No. 3, March 7, 1953, pg. 16-17

Cohen, Harold V., "Observation Post." *TV Digest*, Vol. X, No. 9, April 18, 1953, pg. 12-13

Cohen, Harold V., "Observation Post." *TV Digest*, Vol. XI, No. 4, June 13, 1953, pg. 12-13.

Everett, Anne. *The Museum of Broadcast Communications*, July 2, 2007.

Gooden, Phyllis, "The Sublime Life of a Second Banana." *TV Headliner*, Vol. 3, No. 5, September, 1957, pg. 68.

Lucanio, Patrick and Gary Coville, "The Johnny Jupiter Show." *Filmfax*, No. 34, Aug./Sept. 1992, pg. 50

(No author credited), "Betty Furness, Super-Saleslady." *TV Digest*, Vol. X, No. 2, February 28, 1953, pg. 8-9.

(No author credited), "Bishop Sheen's Monumental Mail." *TV Digest*, Vol. X, No. 7, April 4, 1953, p. 8-9

(No author credited), "Chatterboxing." *TV Digest*, Vol. X, No. 7, April 4, 1953, p. 38.

Websites:

The Museum of Broadcast Communications — Subject Kinescope

Wikipedia — Subjects "Charles Van Doren" and "Quiz Show Scandal"

INDEX

$64,000 Question, The* 83
Actor's Studio 56
Adler, Clyde 72
Admiral Broadway Revue, The 52
AFM 64
AFRA 64
AFTRA 31, 64
Alcoa Hour, The 110
ATE 64
Airplane 98
Allen, Fred 25, 82
Allen, Woody 46
American Theatre Wing, The 36
Amos 'n' Andy 30
Andrews Sisters 65
Andy Griffith Show, The 89, 105
Aparo, Jim 75
Appointment With Adventure 121
Arden, Eve 66
Armchair Theatre, The
   "Underground" 91
Arnaz, Desi 107, 117, 123, 126
Arnell, Peter 43
Arthur Murray Party, The 28, 29
As the World Turns 47, 106
Bacall, Lauren 29
Ball, Lucille 107, 116, 117, 120, 123
Barry, Jack 84
Beat the Clock 83
Begley, Ed Sr. 112, 119
Benny, Jack 21, 25, 64, 112
Benoit, Patricia 27
Berg, Gertrude 30
Berle, Milton 20, 24, 110, 111, 112
Bernard, Tom 21
Beverly Hillbillies, The 37
Bill Nye, the Science Guy 71
Bird Cage, The 35
Bishop, Joey 83
Bitler, Jacqueline 112
Blacklisting 22-23, 32, 115

Bogart, Humphrey 29
Bogart, Paul 52
Bonnie and Clyde 119
Bourgeois, Roland 38
Bourneuf, Philip 53
Boyd, William 123, 126
Breadtime Story 74-75
Brice, Fanny 25
Bridges, Lloyd 81
Broadway Television Theatre
   "Three Cornered Moon" 92
Brothers, Dr. Joyce 83
Brown, Jo 115
Brynner, Yul 23, 35-36, 116-117
Buchanz, Alan 51
Buffalo Bob 27, 72, 112, 118
Buloff, Joseph 38
Burghoff, Herbert 36
Burns and Allen 21, 22, 25
Buttons, Red 24
Buttram, Pat 28
Caesar, Sid 39, 40, 46, 49, 52, 53, 64, 100-101,
   110, 118
Caesar's Hours 52
Cagney, James 105-106
Cantor, Eddie 25, 56
Captain Kangaroo 73
Captain Video and His Video Rangers 72, 102
Carlos, Ernest 36
Carney, Art 99, 121
Carpenter, Carleton 36
Carson, Johnny 110
Cash, Johnny 37
Cassell, Arthur 31
Cavett, Dick 46
CBS Morning Show, The 56
Cerf, Bennett 82, 83
Chambers, Stan 77, 78, 95
Chaney, Lon Jr. 94-95
Chapin, Lauren 32
Chayefsky, Paddy 54, 125

Childress, Alvin 30
City at Night 78
Climax 51, 52, 67, 97
   "Volcano Seat, The" 96
Clooney, Rosemary 46
Cobb, Lee J. 55, 61
Coca, Imogene 39, 40, 52, 53, 100, 110
Coe, Fred 18, 20, 23, 93, 115, 120
Cohen, Harold V. 40, 54
Collyer, Bud 83
Como, Perry 104
Coopersmith, Jerome 68
Coughlin, Kevin 21
Coward, Noel 119
Cowboy Slim 27
Cox, Wally 27
Crompton, Nanci 111
Cronkite, Walter 124
Crosby, Bing 123
Crosby, Lon 95
Cullen, Bill 81, 82, 83, 104
Cummings, Robert 26
Dali, Salvador 82
Daly, John 82, 83
Damon, Les 105
Danger 45, 48, 62, 92, 119
David Rose Orchestra, The 61
Davis, Joan 50
Davis, Madilyn Pugh 107
Days of Our Lives 32
Dean, James 56, 83, 119, 120
DGA 64
Ding Dong School 74
Dixon, John 37
Don Quixote 94
Donahue, Elinor 32
Donehue, Vincent 23, 46
Dougherty, Marion 37, 116, 117
Douglas, Donna 37-38
Douglas, Melvyn 35, 116
Downs, Hugh 42, 118
Duff, Howard 40
Durante, Jimmy 118
Du Mont, Allen 23
Ed Sullivan Show, The 112 (see also *Toast of the Town*)
Ed Wynn Show, The 22
Eight is Enough 31
Erwin, Bill 93, 125

Everett, Anne 23
Family Affair 51
Farnsworth, Philo T. 17
Father Knows Best 32
Faye, Alice 25
Fiscus, Kathy 77-78
Fisk, Jim 75
Foch, Nina 67
Folkine, Vitale 36
Fonda, Henry 29
Foote, Horton 46, 47, 116, 124
Ford, Constance 36
Ford Star Jubilee
   "Bell for Adano, A" 61
Four Star Playhouse 66
Francis, Arlene 82, 83
Frank Sinatra Show, The 65
Frankenheimer, John 40, 52, 63, 124
Franklin, Nancy 31
Freddie Freihofer Show, The 74-75
Freedman, Albert 84
French, Peggy 38, 48
Freund, Karl 123, 126
Frosty Frolics 56
Furness, Betty 25, 41, 87-89, 124
Gabby Hayes Show, The 68
Garner, Peggy Ann 38, 48, 60, 65, 97
Garroway, Dave 110
Garry Moore Show, The 89, 107
Garver, Kathy 51, 97
Gates, Ruth 21
Gateson, Marjorie 31
George, Michael 111
GiGi 42
Gillis, Ann 62
Gish, Dorothy 46-47
Gish, Lillian 47
Gleason, Jackie 47, 99, 121
Going Places 61
Goldbergs, The 30
Goldsmith, Paul 110
Gomer Pyle, USMC 42
Gould, Jack 53
Grady, Don 51, 94, 121
Graham, June 88
Graham, William 118
Grauer, Ben 81
Gray, Billy 32
Greenwood, Pamela 109-110

Griffin, Merv 56, 61, 104-105
Griffith, Andy 56
Guiding Light, The 47
Gunsmoke 81, 112
Hallmark Hall of Fame, The 60
   "Touch of Steel, The" 94
Halloran, Tom 28
Hampton, Walter 119
Hansen, William 46
Harding, Ann 119
Hardwicke, Sir Cedric 67
Harrington, Robert 28
Harris, Robert H. 30
Harvey, Paul 77
Hatfield, Hurd 63
Hawkins, Jimmy 21
Hayden, Jeffrey 52
Hayden, Sterling 40, 63, 124
Hayes, Bill 32, 118
Hayes, Helen 119
Hayes, Richard 38-39
Hayes, Susan Seaforth 32
Hazel Bishop Show, The 104-105
Heckert, Eileen 36
Henderson, Marsha 38
Herbert, Don 71-72
Heston, Charlton 99, 118
Hift (critic) 46
Hill, George Roy 36, 52
Holder, Peter Anthony 106
Holland, Maury 23, 53, 116
Homeier, Skip 68
Honeymooners, The 48, 99
Hope, Bob 37
Horwich, Dr. Frances 74
How the Golden Age of Television Turned My Hair to Silver 89
Howard, Rance 36-37, 59, 64, 95-96, 118, 124
Howdy Doody 27, 72, 73, 75, 105, 110, 112, 119
Howell and Radcliff 101
Hunter, Kim 53
Hyer, Martha 66
I Love Lucy 29, 87, 117, 123, 126
   "Cuban Pals" 107
   "Lucy and Harpo Marx" 107
   "Lucy Makes a Commercial" 107
(I Remember) Mama 20, 21, 30
I've Got a Secret 81-82

Jean, Gloria 60
Johns Hopkins Science Review 103
Jones, Gareth 91
Jory, Victor 99-100
Joyce, Ed 75
Johnny Jupiter 73-74
Kaiser Aluminum Hour, The 124
Kanna, Ralph 75
Karloff, Boris 94
Karnilova, Maria 36
Keeshan, Bob 72, 73, 103-104, 118-119
Keith, Brian 98
Keith, Robert 53
Kennedy Assassination 82
Kerry, Margaret 21
Kiley, Richard 92, 112
Kilgallen, Dorothy 82, 83
Kilgallen, Elinor 116
King and I, The 117
King, June 113
King, Michael 27
King, Wright 7, 9-11, 13, 46, 81, (all bold type) Photos: 10, 42, 47, 51, 62, 68
King, Wright Jr. 81
Kirby Hooton, Claire 50, 59, 119
Kirby, Durwood 30, 89
Kisseloff, Jeff 55
Klugman, Jack 25, 29, 36, 37, 37, 49, 93, 109, 118, 120, 123-124
Knotts, Don 105, 125
Kotar, S. L. 74, 75, 112
Kraft Television Theater 9, 23, 112, 117, 118, 124
   "Man Most Likely, The" 53
   "Most Blessed Woman" 64
   "Paper Foxhole" 37
   "Sheriff's Man" 64
Krampner, Jon 115
Kulik, Buzz 52
Laire, Juddson 21
Lambert, Jack 112-113
Landsberg, Klaus 27, 77, 78-79
Lassie 41, 112
Laudermilk, Sherman 56
Leachman, Cloris 91
Lee, Johnny 30
Lee, Peggy 107
Leigh, Janet 68
Lewis, Jerry 50

Lewis, Sheri and Lambchop 112
Liebman, Max 39
Life of Riley, The 21
Life Is Worth Living 27
Lindgren, Bruce 71
Lockhart, Gene 41
Lockhart, June 41
Lockhart, Kathleen 41
Loeb, Philip 30
Lorne, Marion 27
Lumet, Sidney 48, 92, 116, 120
Lupino, Ida 40-41
Lux Video Theatre 23, 52, 68
Lytell, Bert 31
Man Against Crime 105
Man in the Shadows, The 115
Mandel, Loring 89
Manecke, Ruth 104
Mann, Delbert 23, 52, 54 115
Mann, Iris 21
Marburger, Janet 110
Marburger, Roy 110
March, Hal 83
Marchand, Nancy 54-55
Marlo, Steven 40-41, 52, 63, 106, 120
Marshall, E. G. 55
Martin, Dean 37, 50
Martin, Mary 28, 29
Marx, Harpo 107
Mason, Harry "Bud" 75
Masquerade Party 81
Massey, Raymond 99, 117
Mather, Mack 72
Matinee Theatre 51, 91, 97
McCloud, Catherine 10
Meadows, Audrey 99
Meeker, Ralph 36
Meriwether, Lee 111
Merlin, Jan 94
Mickey Mouse Club, The 121
Minor, Worthington 23, 99, 115
Mission to the World 27
Mister Ed and Me 102-103, 118
Montgomery, Elizabeth 112
Moore, Garry 30, 81, 82
Moore, Tim 30
Morgan, Henry 81, 82, 89
Morgan, Robin 21
Mork and Mindy 73

Morning Show, The 119
Morris, Howard 39, 64, 100-101
Mouseketeers Cubby, Karen, Annette, and Darlene 121
Mr. Adams and Eve 40-41
Mr. Ed 102, 103
Mr. Peepers 27, 120
Mr. Roberts 37
Mr. Wizard 71, 74 (see also *Watch Mr. Wizard*)
Mulligan, Bob 120
Murray, Arthur 29
Murray, Kathryn 29
Murray, Ken 117
My Friend Irma 21
Myerson, Bess 81, 82
NABET-CWA 64
Naked Gun 98
New York World's Fair, The 18, 19
Newman, Paul 56, 100, 120, 125, 126
News at Ten: Fifty Years with Stan Chambers 79
Nickell, Paul 23, 52, 61, 116
Nielsen, Leslie 56, 98
Niven, David 46, 66
Nolan, Kathleen 28
Nugent, Judy 21
Nye, Bill 71
O'Brien, Margaret 68, 109
Odd Couple, The 121
Oetjen, Rev. Marguerite 111
One Man's Family 31, 93
Out There 91
Paar, Jack 110
Page, Geraldine 124
Palance, Jack 53
Paley, William S. 19, 22
Palmer, Betsy 41-43, 51, 54, 62, 81, 82, 93, 119, 121, 123
"Patterns" 112
Pee Wee's Playhouse 74
Penn, Arthur 23, 52, 95, 115, 119
Peppard, George 26, 126
Peter Pan 28-29
Peters, Emily 21, 110
Petrillo Ban 20
Philco Television Playhouse 10, 20, 23, 45, 47, 67, 93, 95, 120
 "Copper, The" 27
 "Crown of Shadows" 61
 "Hear My Heart Speak" 99

"Marty" 54-55, 109
"Shadow of Willie Greer, The" 46, 115
Pilonero, Ted 27, 112
Pine, Philip 116
Pinky Lee Show, The 74
Playhouse 90 52
   "Last Man, The" 40, 63
   "Old Man" 124
   "Requiem For a Heavyweight" 53
   "Time of Your Life, The" 121
Poole, Lynn 103
Post, Ted 52, 116
Post, William Jr. 53
Power, Tyrone 119
Preminger, Otto 115
Presley, Elvis 37
Price is Right, The 83, 104
Producer's Showcase 55, 120
   "Darkness at Noon" 61
   "Peter Pan" 28-29
   "Petrified Forest, The" 29
Pulitzer Prize Playhouse 48
Queen's Messenger, The 18
Quinn, Anthony 10
Quinn, Stanley 23, 116
R K Art School 75
Rae, Claude 72
Randall, Tony 27, 31, 120-121
Randolph, Amanda 30
Randolph, Lillian 30
Reagan, Ronald 25
Red Skelton Show, The 109-110
Reiner, Carl 39, 64, 100
Reiner, Rob 39
Remick, Lee 117
Rennie, Michael 96
Rice, Rosemary 21
Rich, Marian 36
Richman, Helen 40
Richman, Peter Mark 40, 50, 60, 63, 119
Ritchard, Cyril 28
Riva, Maria 117
Robbin, Irvin 56
Robert Montgomery Presents
   "Burtons, The" 41
   "Soldier From the Wars Returning" 105-106
Robinson, Judy 47
Robinson, Larry 30
Romano, Raymond 127

Roosevelt, President Franklin 18
Rough Riders, The 94
Ruggles, Charlie 20, 21
Ruggles, The 20, 21
Saint, Eva Marie 31, 93
Sales, Soupy 72-73
Salmi, Albert 26, 36, 50, 64, 96-97, 100, 118, 126
Salmi, Catherine 97
Sarnoff, David 17, 19, 22
Saturday Night Live 127
Say It With Acting 81
Schaaf, Lillian 31
Schaffner, Franklin 23, 52
Schlitz Playhouse of the Stars, The 65, 68
Scopp, Alfie 72
Scully, Joe 116
Sea Hunt 81
Search For Tomorrow 105
Secret Storm, The 32
Seinfeld, Jerry 127
Serling, Rod 53, 112
Sheen, Bishop Fulton 27-28, 111
Sheridan, Ann 82
Simon, Danny 46
Simon, Neil 46
Singleton, Doris 107
Skelton, Red 21, 28, 109-110
Skipper Frank 27
Smith, Bob 72, 73, 118-119
Smith, Kate 21, 101
Somewhere In Time 93
Spotlights & Shadows 36
Stanley, Kim 60, 118
Stanton, Frank 19
Starlight Theatre 116
Steiger, Rod 36, 49-50, 53-55, 109
Stempel, Herb 84
Stephens, Harvey 66
Steve Allen Show, The 59, 105, 111
Stevens, Robert 116
Stewart, Horace 30
Stone, Harold J. 30
Strother, Rex 38
Studio One 36, 41, 88, 93, 110, 111, 115, 116, 119, 124, 125
   "Abe Lincoln in Illinois" 99
   "Dangerous Years, The" 91
   "Guiulio" 63

"Judgment at Nuremberg" 89
"Julius Caesar" 53
"Laughmaker, The" 121
"Lonely Boy, The" 35, 87
"Paris Feeling, The" 62
Sullivan, Ed 46, 107, 111, 112
Sullivan, Francis L. 65
Sutton, Frank 43-43
Sutton, Toby 42
Swift, Lela 88
Tales of Tomorrow 56
  "Appointment on Mars" 98
  "Universal Solvant, The" 99-100
Taylor, Tom 30
Taylor, Vaughn 73
Tedrow, Irene 21
Tetzel, Joan 67
Texaco Star Theater 20
This is Your Life 64
Thomas, Danny 24
Thomas, Frank Jr. 31
Thompson, Chuck 37
Thorson, Russell 31
Three Sons, The 101
Toast of the Town 112
  "Journey's End" 46
Today Show, The 110
Tom Corbett, Space Cadet 94
Tonight Show, The 94
Tony and Me 120
Townes, Harry 55, 116
Treasury Men in Action 29
A Tree Grows in Brooklyn 38
Trettel, Don 24
Twenty-One 83-85
Twilight Zone, The 81, 93
Two Girls Named Smith 38-39, 48
U. S. Steel Hour, The
  "Bang the Drum Slowly" 110, 124, 126
  "No Time For Sergeants" 56
Van Doren, Charles 84-85
Van Doren, Dorothy 84
Van Doren, Mark 84
Van Dyke, Dick 119
Van Patten, Dick 21, 30
von Furstenberg, Betsy 64, 118
Wade, Ernestine 30
Wade, Warren 92
Wagner, Helen 47, 106

Wallace, Stone 53
Wallach, Eli 120
Wanted, Dead or Alive 81
Watch Mr. Wizard 110
Weaver, Pat 28-29
Welk, Lawrence 95
Welsh, Bill 78
WGA 64
What a Life (The Henry Aldrich Show)" 10, 11
What's My Line? 82-83
Whelan, Kenneth 89-90, 99, 104, 119, 121
Whelan, Susan 104
When Lilies Bloom 118
Williams, Spencer 30
Wood, Peggy 20, 21
Wyatt, Jane 32
Wynn, Ed 25, 53, 118
Wynn, Keenan 53
You Are There
  "Death of Cleopatra, The" 60
  "Final Hours of Joan of Arc, The" 118
Young, Alan 56, 102-103
Young, Robert 32
Your Show of Shows 39, 40, 100, 118
Zworykin, Vladimir 17

OTHER BOOKS BY SANDRA GRABMAN

Spotlights & Shadows: The Albert Salmi Story
Plain Beautiful: The Life of Peggy Ann Garner
Pat Buttram, the Rocking-Chair Humorist

THE MAJOR LIVE TELEVISION SHOWS ON WHICH WRIGHT KING APPEARED

The Ken Murray Show
Lamp Unto My Feet
Starlight Theatre
Pulitzer Prize Playhouse
Schlitz Playhouse of the Stars
Out There
The Gabby Hayes Show
Studio One
Hallmark Hall of Fame
Suspense
Treasury Men in Action
Betty Crocker Star Matinee
Robert Montgomery Presents
Danger
Broadway Television Theatre
Goodyear Television Playhouse
The Philco Television Playhouse
Kraft Television Theatre

BearManorMedia

Can you resist looking at these great titles from Bear Manor Media?

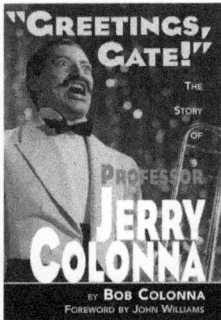

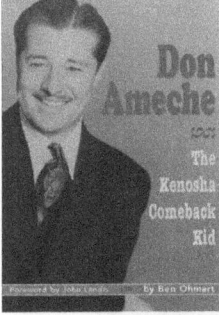

We didn't think so.

To get details on these, and nearly a hundred more titles—visit
www.bearmanormedia.com

You'll be sorry!

...if you miss out.   P.S. Don't be sorry.

www.ingramcontent.com/pod-product-compliance
Lightning Source LLC
Chambersburg PA
CBHW031151160426
43193CB00008B/333